The Future of the Mind

The New Mind's Eye

Jack Huber

Published in this first edition in 2013 by:
Triarchy Press
Station Offices
Axminster
Devon EX13 5PF
United Kingdom

+44 (0)1297 631456
info@triarchypress.net
www.triarchypress.net

A catalogue record for this book is available from the British Library.

Paperback ISBN: 978-1-909470-07-1
Hardback ISBN: 978-1-909470-08-8
ePub ISBN: 978-1-909470-09-5

www.thefutureofthemind.com

Dedication

This book is dedicated to the memory of Don Michael, a dear friend who encouraged me during my early work on this book and insisted I address changes in the mind itself.

Forewarned is Forearmed

The basic premise underlying this book, the behavior of complex adaptive systems, does not seem to be logical—at least not logical by the commonly accepted norms of logic. Cause and effect don't seem to apply; they have little, if any, meaning. The premise is not subject to easy analysis—at least not to analysis supported by conventional mathematics; its non-linear nature is unpredictable and its consequences have been described as chaotic. It requires us to revise our ideas of the self and the ego and diminishes their importance. In so doing, it undermines some psychological ideas and principles that underpin our whole way of thinking about ourselves—at least in the Western world. It seems to defy the basic laws of physics—relationships reach across domains and dimensions. It is philosophically confusing to those on both sides of the 'Descartes issue'. It does not recognize divisions of study into disciplines of expertise—except that of its own.

In short, the basic premise requires the re-perception of just about all we know about the world and ourselves... and the surrender of self to constant re-mashing. If you enjoy that kind of challenge, then I hope you will find the book thought-provoking.

Contents

Acknowledgements

It would have been impossible to write this book without the work of numerous other writers in the diverse fields covered in this book. I am grateful for their work. A few are mentioned in the text, some in the notes at the end of each chapter and many more in the bibliography. The Global Business Network was generous in the working space and in the intellectual stimulation it provided at various times while I was writing this book. I particularly want to thank them for hosting the talk by George Lakoff and Francisco Varela on the subject of embedded knowledge—the talk that started my work on this book.

Robert Horn offered several helpful suggestions on portions of the book. I am particularly indebted to him for the questioning nature of the book. I am grateful for the support of Jay Ogilvy, who, throughout the years of my research and writing, provided thought-provoking and supportive discussions of the mind, complexity theory, and emergence.

Very special thanks must go to Napier Collyns. From the beginning, Napier encouraged me, supporting my interests, reading drafts, suggesting approaches, introducing me to people with related interests, and providing a context for writing and editing. Without Napier, this book would not have been completed. I am also grateful to Napier for the friendship he forged between Don Michael and myself—the inspiration for the focus of this book on the mind.

Last, I am very grateful to my editor, Andrew Carey. His probing questions, indefatigable reading and re-reading, and his inexhaustible patience led to a far more readable book than I brought to him initially.

Finally, no one is to blame for the result except me.

Jack Huber
June 2013

Introduction

Why this Book?

Wherever people discuss the intense connectivity and interaction of the digital age, a profound sense of unease can usually be found. In news accounts and analyses, whether in print or online, in journals, books, blogs and social networks… in whatever flavor of interaction you choose, discussions arise about how we are changing. Whether the focus is on the preoccupation of our children with remote access and digital media, the unrelenting pace of change and competition in work, the increasing digitalization of leisure time, the embrace of ever more remote social life, or even collaborations in science—there is anxiety about what is going on. Not about the modes or the media of interaction we use, but to ourselves. We are concerned about our children. We worry over the pace and intensity. We question changes in the world around us. But underneath all this is the question: what is happening to us? What is happening to our minds? What is happening to our very concept of mind? Have we lost control? Did we ever have control?

Preoccupied with our new gadgets and our new connections, distracted by reports of what we can access and how we can participate… what are we missing? At every step our species is actively creating an environment that is, in turn, influencing our own evolution. But perhaps something even more profound than that is happening. Has this interaction of our nervous systems with cyberous systems gone beyond the simple augmentation of our senses? Have we and our cyberous environment become so integrated that we are as one? Is this intense interaction and cyberous augmentation stimulating the emergence of a new mind? Some scientists are beginning to believe that mind now extends beyond the flesh of self, beyond me. Is this possible?

Why Me?

Ideally, someone competent in many pertinent fields of knowledge would be required to explore these questions. But that would mean leaving the task undone. As Steven Pinker observed in *How the Mind Works*, "At this high altitude there is little difference between a specialist and a thoughtful layperson because nowadays we specialists cannot be more than laypeople in most of our own disciplines, let alone neighboring ones." It is unlikely that I have included all of the most persuasive material here. Nevertheless, it is a beginning.

For me, it began with a small group of people gathered at Global Business Network in Emeryville, California in February, 1994. George Lakoff, Professor of Linguistics at the University of California, Berkeley, and Francisco Varela, Director of Research at the Institute of Neurosciences, École Polytechnique, Paris, were discussing perception, categorization, and how the mind acquires and uses knowledge. Lakoff was interested in how the mind uses what it knows to move into abstract thinking through the use of metaphors. Varela focused on the relationship of the body to the mind. Both were interested in how the mind learns from the external world, how the body learns with the environment.

I was surrounded by people actively bringing us into the high-tech, interactive world. An idea bubbled to the surface. With all the hype about the Internet, the use of computer graphics in the presentation of information, graphical interfaces, interactivity, and virtual reality, were we missing something much more profound? Was all the talk about access, education, and learning missing the point? I read Lakoff's *Fire, Women, and Dangerous Things* and (with Mark Johnson) *Metaphors We Live By*. I read *The Embodied Mind* by Varela, Thompson, and Rosch. I became convinced we were missing a profound change that was seeping through humanity.

Some questions were answered and many more provoked by the work of William Calvin, theoretical neurophysiologist at the University of Washington in Seattle. In a series of books, Calvin explores how environmental changes can influence the evolution of the mind. Furthermore, Calvin believes the changes leading to the future of the mind will be found in the trajectories of changes that reach forward from the past. How has the mind changed? What are those trajectories? How do they operate? How are they linked to changes in the environment?

Is each mind changing its environment as it collaborates with it—and consequently changing itself?

Theoretical biologist and complex systems researcher Stuart Kauffman, in a provocative talk at The Santa Fe Institute, introduced me to emergent properties. Could the self-organization of complex adaptive systems and their emergent properties in some way account for the mind's relationship to the central nervous system and the environment? If so, how long has this relationship been in progress? What are the driving forces in this relationship? Where are they going in the future? What is the future of mind?

That is what this book is all about. Three trajectories of change have been identified and projected into the future of the mind. They are pattern recognition, vision, and post-birth development. That future rests on the continuing co-evolution, self-organization, and collaboration of body and environment, and a mind which emerges from the collaboration of the two. The future of the mind will emerge from the sensual embodiment of the environment now influenced by the mind's own design of that environment. In addition, features which challenge our current understanding of mind— the unknowable dimension of mind and the participation in mind of elements external to the body—will redefine who and what we are.

This book leans heavily on the work of many people in numerous disciplines. What is new is the re-perception of mind itself, using new interpretations of the research and analysis available to both professional, and general, science readers. Both should find this book provocative.

Setting the Stage

What is the significance of being *The Symbolic Species*? What are the consequences of living in *The Interface Culture?* Should we be concerned that *The Singularity is Near*? What is it like to be *Alone Together*, or to be *Wired For Thought*? What does it really mean *When Machines Begin to Think?* What are the implications of *Supersizing The Mind?*[1]

While all of our senses are bombarded with information from our environment, the assault on vision is more intense than any other sense and our vision is supported by more of our neural resources than any other.

Visual information is intense. It encompasses both the specific and the general at the same time. It is both focused and comprehensive. But what if our intense visual absorption—all of those screens we live with and the application of computer-generated information to the mind—actually altered our evolution and led to the evolution of something new? What if these screens, these electronic visual adjuncts, were becoming an extension of the mind—not in the cyborg sense, but in the stream of our own perception? What if, for the first time ever, a species was not simply using the environment, but actually changing the environment in such a way that the environment would, in turn, change the species itself—stimulate the next step in its own evolution? Is that possible? What would it take? Sounds bizarre doesn't it?

For this to happen—for us to start shaping our own evolutionary future—would vision need to be capable of adapting in some manner to the increasing intensity of the information presented by cyber-driven visual displays? And how would the mind need to use this information? What would need to change to make a difference? But even then, how would all of this be translated into inherited characteristics, rather than being re-learned by each generation in turn? Need it be? And if this were possible, how long would it take? Would the early stages be recognizable? Where would it show up first? In children? In what they learn? Or how

---

1   For all references like these, see the Bibliography.

they learn? Or how they use what they learn? Would there be discernible differences in how generations think? Would there be a leap in the ability of people to handle abstractions? Would metaphor change? What would be the differentiating characteristics? Perhaps more important, is this electronic visual stimulation simply the continuation of a longer term phenomenon that we have not hitherto perceived: the mind's use of externally stored and analyzed information? Could the changes progress beyond simple augmentation of the visual sense?

How can we explore these questions? What new perspective is needed? Traditionally, we have analyzed relationships as linear. Effect follows cause in predictable fashion. If only we can capture the sometimes elusive mathematics which describes the relationships, we will understand them and—the ultimate desire—control them! This long tradition of linear analysis and prediction has been reinforced by the introduction of the digital computer.

But what if that perspective is wrong? What are we missing with our egocentric, linear perspectives looking out from within our own neurosystems? Until recently we have simplified our analyses and understanding of ourselves by refusing to accept that we are part of everything around us. But, increasingly, we are finding the relationships of which we are a part to be nonlinear. Cause and effect are not so clear. Even nature refuses to follow our simple linear logic. We have various names to characterize these newly identified relationships: non-linear systems, chaos theory, network theory, complexity theory, and complex adaptive systems. These systems are all around us—in political, economic, biological, cosmological... and electronic settings. We ourselves are comprised of these non-linear systems, the most awesome of which is our brain.

I want to start by re-perceiving these questions in the context of complex adaptive systems—beginning with a brief survey of nature's relentless self-organizing. Complex adaptive systems, perhaps counter-intuitively, lurk behind the seemingly stable façade of everyday life and of life itself—from cells to consumers, from the weather to rush-hour traffic... and from vision to the mind. Yet, science is only now beginning to appreciate them.

There is an interesting phenomenon associated with these systems: emergent properties. These properties emerge from the interactions of the elements of a system and cannot be predicted from an analysis of either the elements or their interactions. Some in science have come to believe that the mind is an emergent property of the collective systems comprising the central nervous system. What of those participating systems outside of 'me'? Do they also participate in the emergence of mind? There are those in science who believe they do.

In the language of complex adaptive systems, the mind is in the midst of a phase-shift. What does that mean? Economics gives us an example. In economic theory, there is a simple relationship between the price of a good and the demand for it. Over a wide range of values for price and demand, this relationship holds. But occasionally a redefining event occurs in the marketplace and the fundamental relationship changes. Following a disruptive change in supply—a new and different source of supply—there comes a shift in demand, accompanied by a shift to a new continuum. Manufacturing augmented crafts. Automobiles supplemented horses. Television augmented radio and movies. Wireless joined wire line. Each time there was a redefining event in the self-organization of the economic system, the relationships among the parts changed.

Such a redefining event occurred in the construct of the mind about 50,000–100,000 years ago. The mind self-reorganized! We see the consequences in the record left behind by our ancestors. Sophisticated art, lurking in caves, appears as if out of nowhere. Adornment of the person, of everyday apparel, increasingly sophisticated icons of worship, and even the decoration of everyday utensils—they all suddenly litter the archaeologist's landscape. This is a mind very unlike the one preceding it. We shall see just how different. The elements enabling the emergence of mind, operating on the eons-long time scale of nature are still shifting the mind to a new continuum. We are still within the swirl of change. Will we belong to the new continuum or the old? Are we still members of the *Homo sapiens* species today?

In order to understand where the mind will go, we must first understand how it came to be. That may not be easy since science begins from what our mind looks like today. It may also be unsettling to our notion of self, which we value so highly. Our species is egocentric. Science is filled with clues to the future of mind—books, papers, research—but, with few exceptions, they address mind only in the singular state of 'me,' and only in a linear fashion. "Me, Myself, and I" has been celebrated in song by everyone from Billie Holiday to Beyoncé to Sho Baraka. Yet we are not simply 'me,' we are part of families, groups, political and economic systems, cultures, and perhaps most importantly, systems of technologies. Today we are members of a web embracing not only all of us but the technology we create. We interact with one another and with technology at an increasingly frenetic pace. We have augmented the capabilities of our brains with enormous external capabilities. The external augmentation of our neural systems is not new. It began eons ago with perhaps something as simple as a pile of rocks, or a deliberately broken tree branch—external memories of locations, events, or direction. These processes of augmentation and interaction continue today. But does it stop simply with augmentation?

The future of the mind appears in three evolutionary trajectories operating through millennia: pattern recognition, vision, and post-birth development. They are inexorably changing who and what we are... changing the very nature of mind. They are independent, yet inextricably bound together.

In **Part One**, we explore the progressive increase in the ability of natural systems to recognize patterns, take action based on patterns, and use patterns in cognition. Our ability to compare different environmental disturbances—to observe patterns in the environment—enabled metaphor-based cognition. And increased sophistication in the acquisition and use of patterns led to the emergence of an integrated realm of subjectivity—the self.

In **Part Two**, we examine the power of vision to enrich the acquisition and evaluation of patterns, the extension of vision by synthetic augmentation, and the education of vision by post-birth development—both natural and cyberous.

Pattern recognition and vision arise from our biology. The ability to see and recognize patterns is contained in the genes passed down by our ancestors after interaction and adaptation with the environment. A special case of pattern recognition, metaphor, is of particular interest.

In **Part Three**, we learn to appreciate the profound implications of electronically augmented post-birth development to the self-organizing and functioning of neural systems. In post-birth development, knowledge and skills acquired by our ancestors, and today incubated by the technology in which we are immersed, are passed on to us within culture—within a system that transcends us individually. With the augmentation of synthetic systems, the cognitive power of metaphor is no longer constrained by neural capacity or by the experience of self.

Part Four explores the future of the mind produced by these three trajectories—pattern recognition, vision, and post-birth development. Are there limitations in the tendencies of change that we explore? Have we appropriately defined mind? We will explore these questions and suggest three futures of mind:

1. **Unknowable Mind.** Our minds are already engaged in activity about which we know only the consequences, if that. We don't know how insights, ahaas! and that language so essential to science itself—metaphor—come about. We are also increasingly exposed to cyberous translations of phenomena beyond human experience—the real unknowable. What is next as the augmentation of technology becomes ever more intense? What *is* mind when technology, about which we are seldom fully aware, participates in the emergence of mind? What does it mean to me to have a mind that is more unknowable than that of my ancestors?

2. **Absentee Mind.** Is it valid to identify as ours, all of those remote memories we can now access with a movement of the cursor or the swipe of a finger? Is it valid to constrain our definition of mind to only those systems of flesh within us? Einstein once said "Never memorize what you can look up in books." Indeed, why encumber the flesh with what can be done collaboratively with silicon or in the Cloud? Remote, absentee participants in mind are increasing. What will that mean to me?

3. **Transcendent Mind.** Is mind still singular? Was it ever, or was that simply a convenient way of evading the messy complexity of the systems of which we are a part? Don't we observe emergence in societies, in cultures, in technology? Is it really useful to pretend that what we so jealously guard as our own, our self, would be the same without the participation of the systems in which we interact as elements? Where does 'self' fit in all of this? What will it mean to me to participate in a collective mind—a mind that transcends me?

As we follow the three trajectories of pattern recognition, vision, and post-birth development through time we will come face-to-face with a profound fact. Mind may be important to us, but it is not important to the self-organizing of nature. It is simply a consequence.

There isn't space to present detailed, complete arguments in support of each idea explored here. Instead, I present the ideas, re-perceived, in a framework designed to explore the evolution of the mind in such a way as to reveal potential for the future of the mind. I present ideas from several disciplines and numerous individuals. Only a few sources are referenced in the text. More are suggested in the section of additional reading at the end of each chapter. Many sources, helpful but more linear in approach, are included in the bibliography.

Continuing observations and developments on *The Future of The Mind* may be found at www.thefutureofthemind.com.

CHAPTER 1
Complexity and Environment

I begin this book with an overview of complexity theory because I believe the mind to be an emergent property of complex adaptive systems: our nervous systems together with those systems of our environment. How can that be?

Have you ever stepped in dog vomit? No, not the consequence of Fido's indiscretions, but the slime mold you may find scuffing through old leaves. Known within its community of friends as *Fuligo septica*, like many slime molds, the cells of this species are independent, but may get together for a walk through the leaves, and certainly for dinner. They may just as likely degenerate into their own diaspora, going their own way. When they do get together they look and move like a gigantic ameba. But if you step in one it's just as disgusting as your dog's indiscretion! So why am I starting this book talking about dog vomit? Because *Fuligo septica* is a beautiful illustration of a complex adaptive system.

The weather is another example of a complex adaptive system. In 1987, James Gleick's book *Chaos: Making a New Science* was published. It caused a sensation among ordinary readers interested in science. It splashed all over best-seller lists and was widely reviewed. It brought to the public a glimpse of the weirdness that supports everyday life and life itself. Gleick explained how Lorenz, a climatologist, first brought us face-to-face with the phenomenon of complexity theory through his study of the weather. Gleick quotes Douglas Hofstadter as saying, "It turns out that an eerie type of chaos can lurk just behind a façade of order—and yet, deep inside the chaos lurks an even eerier type of order."

It seems that dog vomit and the weather have something in common. They are both complex adaptive systems. Complex adaptive systems also underlie the three trajectories provoking the future of the mind: the processes of pattern recognition, vision, and post-birth development. It is no exaggeration to say that if evolution is the process of change, then complex adaptive systems are the means of the process.

Earth has passed through numerous periods from the Precambrian to the present including the most celebrated of all—the Jurassic with its fearsome dinosaurs. Countless species have come and gone. Today, there are millions of species, all with their own way of making a living. On the eons-long time scale of evolution, nature seems to reorganize the players every so often. Within the processes of nature, there seems to be an urge to reorganize. There is no outer direction for this organization. It is best described as self-organization. It is this relentless process of self-organizing that lurks behind the three trajectories that I am discussing and behind the future of the mind.

Twenty-five years after Gleick's *Chaos*, there is as yet no comprehensive theory of these complex systems. But like the elephant partially explored and described by the blind men, these systems have been described in various ways by different scientific disciplines: non-linear systems, chaos theory, complex adaptive systems, network systems, and emergent systems are some of the perspectives given to them. I will use the term 'complex adaptive system' because adaptation is important to this story. For the sake of brevity, I will abbreviate the term to CAS (with CASs as its plural).

But be warned! CASs can seem counter-intuitive if not incongruous. We have an innate confidence in the regulated processes of life—cause and effect flow everywhere. Perhaps, as Douglas Hofstadter suggested, CASs are a little unsettling. Rudderless, without direction or objective—except for an unceasing urge to reshape themselves, to self-organize and self-organize and self-organize... ad infinitum. Yet, they are where this story begins. CASs are all around us. They *are* us and they *are* the environment. They adapt to change in their environment while becoming the changing environment of other CASs. They are a fundamental part of this story and the future of the mind.

CASs are distinct from systems that are only complicated. I may cut the grass with a lawn mower—a relatively complicated machine of numerous interconnected, interacting systems and parts, including starter, fuel, ignition, exhaust, propulsion, cutting, and grass handling. No matter what the conditions or the weather—hot or cold, snow or rain, or the terrain—smooth, flat, or filled with gullies—the machine will attempt to cut. No matter what is encountered—grass or weeds, bricks or twigs, flowers or garden hose—the lawn mower will do the same thing. It will attempt to cut whatever I put in its path. The lawn mower just sits there through rain, snow, heat, or cold, unless I move it. It does not adapt to change in its environment. But the grass, also complicated in nature, is a self-organizing system. It changes with no outside or centralized direction. It adapts to the stimulation of seasonal change. Grass withers in the face of dryness to preserve its future, grows with nutrients, reproduces, and goes dormant in the cold, saving itself for recovery in the warmth. Over eons of time, grass has adapted to changing environments.

The lawn mower is complicated. The grass is a complex adaptive system.

So why are we interested in CASs? These systems can be found at the cellular level and every other level all the way up to ourselves... and beyond! They are hierarchical. What do I mean by that? We normally think of hierarchies as levels of cooperation or collaboration within an organization like a church, or a firm, or an educational institution. In the case of CASs, the hierarchies come about through an interesting aspect of their organization. A CAS, once formed, is then available to be used as an element in the formation of a higher-order CAS. These higher-order levels can carry on without limit. Thus we have cells organized into systems into organs into people. We have individuals organizing into consumers or producers, groups into markets, markets into economies. They are all around us! And we need to understand a few things about this CAS phenomenon before proceeding.

So what makes up these systems? How do they work? If they are not fully understood by science, how can they be useful? There are several known aspects of these phenomena that are of interest to us.

- They are comprised of independent, basic elements—ranging from cells to consumers to galaxies.

- These elements self-organize in response to changes in the environment.

- The self-organizations balance between stability and chaos—on the edge of chaos.

- They only self-organize into possibilities adjacent to their initial conditions.

- They harbor an unpredictable property: emergence.

It is in this property of emergence that we will find the future of the mind.

The Basic Elements

All CASs are comprised of building blocks, independent elements interacting with one another for the benefit of the whole. You scratch my back and I'll scratch yours? Well, it is not quite that simple. Together, the interacting elements are better able to interact with their environment— better than any individual element could do on its own, *and* they collaboratively develop a capability for manipulating that environment for the good of the CAS and for the good of each of the elements. Even so, CASs are not necessarily optimal. Typically, they are just good enough, good enough to persist, good enough to survive, and good enough to multiply. I will explore this characteristic of CASs throughout the book.

The basic elements comprising a CAS need not be identical so long as they relate on a common basis. This characteristic of the element is illustrated by the object-oriented construct used in computer programming, where objects belong to a substitutable class no matter what their other characteristics, *so long as they retain the characteristics of the class.* They may differ in size, scale, or properties. So long as they relate with the same 'language,' function together in a common interest and maintain their integrity, the elements may be of any mix. They need not be 'living,' or mineral, or even sentient, (though they may be all of these and more). The elements comprising economies and societies—both CASs—demonstrate this aspect of the elements of CASs. CASs can include many disparate elements—even other CASs.

The interfaces among elements determine the manner of exchange—the modality of interaction among the elements in a system. In an economy it may be currency; in a brain, dopamine. This modality both supports and constrains the relationship of the elements and contributes to the simplicity of the relationships. These interfaces support feedback for two-way interaction and exchange. The most familiar example of this modality constraint is our senses. We smell odors, not light.

These interactions can be seemingly chaotic. Elements may participate in multiple CASs simultaneously. It's like belonging to a poker club, a bridge club, and a pinochle club… on the same night, in the same room, at adjacent tables. Elements need only adhere to the protocol of each of the CASs in which they participate. This property is evident in economies where individuals can be manufacturing workers, service providers, consumers, or facilitators of the interaction of others. Multiple roles are also apparent in societies, and in the central nervous system. Disintegration, or perhaps disengagement, occurs when participation in a CAS leads to conflict among the functions of the elements. We see this in bankruptcies, corporate buyouts, revolutions, mental disturbances, and the ultimate cellular disengagement—death.

There's more. Since any element in an environment is eligible to participate in a CAS, the CASs *themselves* participate in relationships with other CASs, self-organizing into an endless potential of layers or hierarchies. In higher order systems within hierarchies, the interfaces may extend deep into the systems and be comprised of other CASs. The hierarchies of interaction can be limitless—important to the future of the mind.

A World of Elements Responding to Change

These systems are all around us. They nurture us. They shape us. They comprise us.

CASs are opportunistic, adapting to change and to stimulation from without. Each CAS functions in the context of its own environment. It is subject to the influence of that environment and self-organizes in response to changes in that environment—but on its own terms. The availability of new or changed elements, the disappearance or modification of elements by the environment, all represent opportunities or threats stimulating self-organization.

Since CASs self-organize as elements of the environment, comprised of elements of the environment, and in response to disturbances in the environment, this self-organization reflects the environment. Self-organizations are consequences of stimulation by the environment; they are an integral *part* of the environment. The current state of a CAS reflects the culmination of all previous self-organizations, all previous responses to the environment. The structure of the CAS represents its response to the environment.

As a CAS changes in response to stimulation or opportunities, it also becomes the changed environment encountered by other CASs. It *is* the environment to other CASs. The relationships and patterns of self-organized systems change as the environmental circumstances do, and environmental circumstances change even as CASs do. In every sense, the self-organizations of CASs reflect their environment and are part of

THE FUTURE OF THE MIND

the environment of other CASs. They co-evolve.

Self-organization at one level of a hierarchy may or may not cause reorganization in other levels of the hierarchy, depending on whether or not the elements in other levels change. We see this in economies and societies. There may be changes within a business, or an industry, or a new set of laws to cope with societal changes, yet the economy—or the societal relationship—persists.

Living on the Edge

Chaos is a term encountered in the study of CASs. Complex adaptive systems encompass both stability and change. They exist at the transition between orderly systems with stability and those that are chaotic in behavior. They truly skirt the edge between stability and chaos. CASs are restless, seemingly without discipline. But there are limits to this restlessness.

CASs are governed by their own emergent rules. The rules for each arise from within and are used by the elements participating for the benefit of the CAS as a whole and the individual elements comprising it. Yet CASs need integrity. When an environmental influence provokes change that is not within the scope of the existing system, the system disintegrates. Poof goes the CAS! The independent elements are then freed into the environment, available for new self-organizations, new CASs. The assets, competitive advantages, skilled workers, trade secrets of commercial organizations in bankruptcy, are dispersed to other organizations capable of using them in their systems. Mergers and acquisitions often 'spin off' unwanted or unusable functions. The chemicals in the cellular makeup of our bodies return to the environment in death.

This brings us to autopoiesis. Autopoiesis, defined by Maturana and Varela, is the process of becoming. According to Maturana and Varela, autopoietic systems literally pull themselves up by their bootstraps and are continually self-producing. The only product of their organization is themselves and there is no distinction between the producer and the product. Sound crazy? Well, as we used to say, "you are one." This process, and every CAS, is constrained both by past structures—by the history of previous self-organizations—and by the need to maintain ongoing structural integrity from moment to moment. Otherwise there is an end to becoming. Stability—no change—is death. Chaos is the collapse of system integrity—also death. Self-organizations and reorganizations that take place within a system while maintaining the integrity of that system operate at the edge of chaos and are said to have the property of autopoiesis: becoming is a process without an end.

This can have unexpected consequences. On the one hand, CASs can have the attributes of both stability and chaos. Well, maybe not simultaneously, but almost. On the other hand, tracing the path of a CAS through history might give the impression that it is seeking a direction—an objective—when it is simply following the path of least resistance through a series of opportunistic self-organizations, moving from one set of environmental conditions to another, and to another, and to another.

These systems can also spontaneously self-organize into sub-systems—into a division of labor. If we consider that these systems are constantly seeking new possibilities at all levels of a hierarchy, these self-organizations into sub-systems are simply moves into adjacent possibilities.

Initial Conditions, Adjacent Possibilities, and Adaptation

What are initial conditions and adjacent possibilities? Initial conditions are just what they say they are. They are the conditions before a change takes place—in whatever. After a change, the new conditions become the initial conditions for the next change. As a CAS self-organizes repeatedly, new initial conditions will arise repeatedly. Change can take place only into adjacent possibilities. They are possible only because they are one step away, adjacent to the initial conditions.

Imagine you are standing on a busy street corner with a traffic light, walk-wait signs, numerous pedestrians, and lots of traffic. Those are your initial conditions. That's where you are. You can obey the traffic signals, walk into the traffic, or walk in another direction. You can bump into or avoid the pedestrians, or dodge the cars and jay-walk. Or you can just stand there. Those are your adjacent possibilities. That's what you can do given where you are. Whatever you do, that becomes your new set of initial conditions for your next move: a move into a set of adjacent possibilities surrounding your new set of initial conditions.

The possibilities adjacent to the current state further limit the self-organizing options available to any CAS, substantially reducing the operation of randomness.

Another aspect of CASs is of particular interest. There is no going back. A CAS self-organizing into an adjacent possibility then resides in that new possibility with its own initial conditions for the next self-organization: the residual structure of the self-organization constitutes the beginnings for the next one. The adjacent possibilities presented from that vantage point do not include the previous state. If I cross the street, I am no longer on the same corner. If I remain on the corner, the traffic conditions will have changed. My adjacent possibilities will have changed. Been there, done that! The environment has moved on. That street corner has a completely different set of opportunities once a choice is made—or not. Traffic and pedestrians change. The signals change. The interaction of all the participants is at a different point. The opportunities are different. The previous state is not within reach. As a consequence, the sequence of initial conditions and adjacent possibilities traversed by self-organizations may not lead to an optimal organization. Suboptimal self-organizations are more likely than optimal ones. An illustration of this characteristic is the man standing among several hills. He is simply told to walk uphill. What are the chances of his reaching the highest peak among all the hills? Once he starts up a low rising hill, there is no turning back... just walk uphill.

Surprisingly, a hierarchy of simple *if-then* rules can lead to complex behavior. An example given by Stuart Kauffman in the study of CASs in biology cited the operation of bacteria. *If* bacteria encounter an increasing flow of glucose, *then* they move toward it. In a noted software program, 'Boids', three simple rules lead to behavior emulating the practice of birds when they flock together. In a hierarchy of decisions, *if-then* rules can be very powerful. As these systems constantly self-organize in response to environmental disturbances, they are adapting to those disturbances.

This same characteristic is evident in the operation of the human central nervous system. The brain is composed of a multitude of sub-systems operating in almost limitless relationships and hierarchies, each subject to the influence of its own environment—including the body and other parts of the brain.

Emergence

Of particular note—and of some mystery—is the fact that these systems have an unpredictable property that emerges from the connections and interactions of the elements in the relationship. It is as if the relationship reaches a critical mass, and—boom—a phase transition occurs. Something emerges that is qualitatively different from the sum of the parts. This emergent property is not predictable from an examination of the individual elements, nor of the connections among those elements.

Consider the movement of automobiles in an urban area. The elements interacting are the individual automobiles, the rules are manifested in the signage and signaling, and in the actions of the drivers. An examination of the elements alone would not disclose the property that emerges from the system—traffic, sometimes stable sometimes chaotic. It is this property of emergence that is most important to the future of the mind.

Today, many basic elements available for self-organization are created by ourselves—the very systems self-organizing. These elements are as primitive as generation-specific adornment and as sophisticated as online social media and search engines. These elements are systems in themselves, with their own environmental stimulation and self-organization—systems we are creating. While it is unusual for a species to create an environment that then brings about subsequent change in that species, it is not new. Beavers build dams to create lakes for their homes. Corals build reefs for their footing. What is new is that the elements influencing the change are not just material. They are cyberous: machine-oriented, electronic in nature. Underlying them are the multiple dimensions of the Internet and the continuing connectivity of ever more sophisticated mobile devices. We are always in touch. Most importantly, these electronic elements are complementary to the three eons-long paths of adjacent possibilities that I mentioned earlier. These three sets of adjacent possibilities are still being explored by the CAS that is made up of us humans: pattern recognition, vision, and post-birth development. These three 'trajectories' in evolution need some exploration before examining the future of the mind and the contribution these forces make to that future.

Suggested Additional Reading for Chapter 1

For an introduction to complexity theory and how it has been revealed by several different disciplines, see Mitchell Waldrop's *Complexity: the Emerging Science at the Edge of Order and Chaos*, and Melanie Mitchell's *Complexity: a Guided Tour* which provides a current overview of complexity theory. John Holland in *Hidden Order: How Adaptation Builds Complexity*; and Stuart Kauffman in *At Home in the Universe: the Search for the Laws of Self-organization and Complexity* provide a more in-depth exploration of complexity theory. Terrance Deacon, in

Incomplete Nature: How Mind emerged from Matter, reviews the evolution of the concept of emergence. In *The Emergence of Everything: How the World Became Complex*, Harold Morowitz examines emergence in 28 levels from the primordial to urbanization.

Niche Construction: the Neglected Process in Evolution, by John Odling-Smee *et al* presents environmental modification by species as a complementing force to adaptation and selection by the environment, and discusses feedback in evolution. Humberto Maturana, in an essay entitled *Biology of Cognition* in the book *Autopoiesis and Cognition: The Realization of the Living*, by Humberto Maturana and Francisco Varela, provides a window onto self-organizing CASs as both biological unities and as simple elements in an environment of interacting systems. Humberto Maturana and Francisco Varela in *The Tree of Knowledge*, provide a basis for the cohesiveness of these systems—autopoiesis. Len Fisher, in *The Perfect Swarm: The Science of Complexity in Everyday Life*, explores group adaptation in the context of complex adaptive systems.

Emergence: Contemporary Readings in Philosophy and Science, edited by Mark Bedau and Paul Humphreys, provides a discussion of emergence from various philosophical and scientific sources. Three perspectives of emergence are provided by John Holland's *Emergence: From Chaos to Order*; Steven Johnson's *Emergence: The Connected Lives of Ants, Brains, Cities and Software*; and *The* 'Mind of The Swarm,' a short article by Erica Klarreich in the November 25, 2006 issue of *Science News*. James Gleick's popular book of a few years past, *Chaos: Making a New Science*, provides an appropriate visual introduction to complexity theory and the property of emergence.

PART ONE

Pattern Recognition
A Hierarchy of Systems and Interfaces

In Part One we will explore pattern recognition. Pattern recognition is a principal force underlying the future of the mind. It is the first of three we will explore on our way to the future of the mind.

Pattern recognition began as the 'ante-up' of survival. Pattern recognition is a hierarchy of complex adaptive systems employing a dizzying array of interfaces and interactions. It is essential to the proper monitoring and governing of an organism's internal state and its relationship with the environment. It is the foundation of mind, as we know it.

We will explore the seemingly aimless wandering of this self-organizing capability: the monitoring and governing functions essential to survival; increasing sensitivity to disturbances in the environment; the coupling of favored reactions with selected patterns; the emergence and influence of 'feelings'; and the importance of encounters with light. Then we will explore the wandering into a centralized, collaborative system of systems, the brain.

CHAPTER 2

Perception

You're walking down the street in a busy city, surrounded by a cacophony of sounds—people talking and traffic blaring, odors tempting or disgusting, and lights flashing—*buy, watch out, see me*. You are talking to friends while texting even as your ear bud messages your psyche. And marvel of marvels, you are walking, too. If you are really feeling cool, you may be bouncing in your walk. (Chewing gum? Well, maybe not.) Every day is filled with perception. We taste. We smell. We hear. We see. We touch. All at once and seldom with confusion. Perception is the beginning and the end of life, and of this story. Perception is our connection to systems outside of our own.

We are interested in perception because: it is an active participant in mind, it is our first encounter with CASs on the way to the future of the mind, and it defines aspects of mind we must consider in any future of the mind.

This chapter is also about interfaces of a more familiar nature than the abstract ones used to describe the interactions inherent in CASs. Our own. These interfaces are not conceptually different from the ones we examined in Chapter 1, but they belong to us.

This chapter is rooted in the world of our immediately lived experience, as we live it, prior to any thoughts about our living it. We depend on this world of experience without necessarily paying it much attention. Yet our experience with this world is always relative to our place in it. This is the world in which we participate as we live. The places where we participate are at our boundaries.

'Perception' is the term I use to describe the way in which we recognize patterns. Perception is the means of pattern recognition. 'Sensation' is the term I use to describe our interface with environmental disturbances. Sensation is a precursor of perception. We define sensations as the transactions with the environment that take place at the boundary of an organism—what is happening to me. Perception is about making sense of what is happening out there, as deduced from what is happening to me in the context of what is happening out there. Clinical research supports this distinction between the neuronal systems for the two aspects of experience—sensation and perception. They are both complex adaptive systems stimulated by the environment. These two, the organism's transactions (in the form of sensations) and registrations (in the form of perceptions), imply dimensions, boundaries that define the organism and its capabilities. These boundaries, and what is contained within them, provide a reference for whatever is registered as a consequence of our 'transactions' with the environment. I will explore these characteristics of the two systems in this chapter.

Stimuli excite sensations before perception can register what is happening. Walk into a dark, strange room and turn on a light. You experience brightness and color by way of sensation. It takes additional time and evaluation to perceive what the light and color signify. Sensations include much that we never evaluate in perception. We walk through familiar surroundings sensing all of the colors and shapes on our retinas, while only a few of the objects are registered in perception. We walk down the street bouncing and rolling from foot to foot, sensing the unevenness of our motions, yet perceiving (or registering) none of it unless we stumble.

In fact, what perception registers is not so much the environment *per se* as disturbances caused by that environment. Perception registers each environmental disturbance as a self-organizing neuronal pattern. These residual patterns provide a basis for matching, classifying, and reacting to subsequent interactions. Perception is the threshold of pattern recognition and mind, but is limited by the interactions taking place at boundaries, the nature of the boundary structure, and the systems confirming those interactions.

I will use sensation and interaction interchangeably—whichever conveys the clearest meaning in context. Similarly, I will use perception and registration interchangeably.

We will explore four important characteristics of these two systems: boundaries; modalities; residual patterns; and feedback giving rise to a subjective present, my 'now.' Then we will explore the implications of these to our story: the separation of subject from disturbance—'me' and 'not me'—a subjective reference, perception without sensation, and ownership.

Some of the issues explored here will surface again as we consider the future of the mind.

Boundaries

One of the powerful aspects of mind is that the world in which we live and move seems so seamless! But consider how important are the beginnings and the ends—the boundaries of things. As I sit here, there is obviously a boundary between me and the chair on which I sit. I gaze through the window—itself a boundary between the inside and the outside of the room, and I see flowers, trees, buildings, people—all enclosed in boundaries. It is our constant encounter with these boundaries that is life as we live it.

Boundaries define what belongs together—in a CAS they are self-defined by the self-organization of the system. Without boundaries there is no integral whole. Boundaries are actively maintained and participate in the system they define. My skin is a boundary of my body. It defines what forms part of me physically—and what does not. It participates in, and is maintained by, the system it defines. My skin is a fully participating, maintained, and nourished, boundary element of my body. An organism's response to a stimulus at the boundary is an essential part of the boundary's participation in the organism.

Good and bad things (transactions) happen at boundaries. There is an advantage to increasing the good and avoiding the bad. Once the transactions have been registered in perception, sharing those registrations with collaborating elements would be an advantage, too: the ability to move toward, or away from disturbance—perhaps a simple reflexive response to heat on the skin—*if* heat is sensed, *then* move to increase it. In this sense, the boundary of the collaborating elements—the skin—began participating with an environment that has distinct characteristics which match distinct boundary sensitivities such as touch or smell. Participation is an important aspect of perception that is often overlooked—the experience of an active interaction between the organism and the environment. Participation is the frontline of co-evolution, of evolving together. This relationship will increasingly manifest itself in the future of the mind.

Boundaries have modalities of exchange with the environment.

Modalities

Just as Texas has its river, gulf and survey lines, boundaries are composed of elements each of which has a unique structure—its modality for exchange. We smell odors, hear sounds, see light, feel touch, and so on.

The sensation of each boundary element is of a form determined by that modality. We can't smell light. Perception begins with the molecular and neural structure of the boundary—the modality of the sensation, the 'modality' indigenous to the interface, the structure in which the transaction takes place. These are themselves CASs. Sensations have co-evolved with the environment and perception has co-evolved with sensations. If you can't see it (sensation), you can't duck (perception/response)!

The modality of a perception is integrally bound to the structural form of the sensation. A transaction of an environmental disturbance at the retina, once registered as something 'seen' will not subsequently be recalled as something smelled. It will forever be bound to the transaction at the retina and its structural form of transaction. The self-organizing response to a visual disturbance is bound to the retina. The resulting neural pattern is of the retinal disturbance. The essence of perception is both boundary location and structural modality. We see the light in our eyes, not the touch on our toes.

The nature of our boundaries and the environment together define the nature of the transactions that will take place and limit the subsequent self-organizing of the perceptual systems. Yet these systems, constrained as they are to modalities, are adequate for distinguishing a rainbow of colors, the range of sounds produced by a symphony orchestra, the tastes of a gourmet dinner, or the many textures found in the forest... or in a clothing store. The nature of our boundaries' modalities affect our participation with the environment and the development of our minds.

There are three processes at work:

1. There is the actual physical disturbance at the boundary where two systems interact in a transaction. Your thumb interacts with the end of a hammer—your thumb absorbs the impact and the hammer stops its motion: a transaction involving an exchange of energy.

2. The transaction is registered. A neural pattern self-organizes because of the sensation—the environmental disturbance of the system—and remains as a residual state for subsequent transactions and self-organizations. This self-organization is a registration of the sensation; it is a perception.

3. The registration confirms the disturbance at the boundary—in the modality of the boundary. Yes, you really did hit your thumb! That self-organized neural pattern registering the transaction will be there as a set of initial conditions—as a memory, we would say—for use the next time you use a hammer.

There are sub-modalities, too. The 'neural registration' of sight records not simply light, but colors of light. We characterize an association between the 'sub-modality' and the pattern of the sensation registered as 'feelings.' Red light tends to excite us and blue light tends to calm us. Itches are irritating and tickles pleasurable. Sweet tastes are pleasing and rotten tastes revolting. While Marshall McLuhan is often quoted as saying "the medium is the message," he also said, "the medium is the massage," more appropriate for our story. The character of the disturbance itself—whether physical or cerebral—is the medium. It is the massaging, the change, that is the medium. Stasis means nothing. It is this medium of massage on which we depend for so much.

This sub-modal quality is an aspect of perception I will return to in subsequent chapters, as modalities outside our bodies join the collaboration of our nervous systems.

Residual Patterns

Our perceptions of environmental disturbances take the form of patterns. I will use the word pattern to signify a residual condition or state of the nervous system that results from, or coincides with, a stimulus. It does not imply an image. Rather, it signifies that some self-organizing event has occurred in one or more neural system, and that the consequence is retained as an altered, residual condition in that neural system. The registration of each new disturbance begins with the residual patterns of previous self-organizations—these residual patterns form the initial conditions within which the neural systems operate. The patterns accumulate and overlap. They intersperse, repeat, and cancel. As patterns repeat, the connections and interactions grow stronger and more durable. As patterns overlap, new relationships self-organize. These neuronal patterns have the properties of CASs. To a stranger, it is just one more self-organized mess. But 'I' know what that mess means. It represents my experience of and with the environment around me.

Initially, sensations and perceptions were both located in the boundary. Perhaps the closest such system remaining in humans is the response of the eye to bright light. A bright light directed into the eye causes the contraction of the pupil, protecting the retina by limiting the intensity of the light stimulating the retina. Self-organizations were limited to those integral to the sensation site. Each system evolved for a distinct mode of disturbance. There was one for vision, or smell, or whatever—but not a single, integrated system. They responded individually. I will explore these responses and their implications in subsequent chapters.

In the restless exploration intrinsic to CASs, the different modal systems moved through adjacent possibilities drawing closer to one another and achieving greater collaboration, while drawing away from their related transaction sites. There is more information in cross-modality registrations. There are more options for response, more opportunities for collaboration among the different types of transactions with the environment: better perceptions of what is happening, better responses to disturbances… improved survival rates.

Eventually, a central location for the patterns of registration emerged, facilitating cross-modal collaboration. Integrating the sight and sound of a threat was more useful. This central location became a new environment in itself, a cerebral environment complete with cerebral boundaries for transactions, registrations, and confirmation—a set of CASs capable of forming patterns and hierarchal systems among themselves without external disturbance. These neural registrations also collectively provide a model of the state of the body at any given moment in time. This inner model of the body became a surrogate for the real body. I will return to this surrogate.

This serendipitous self-organizing into a central nervous system is evident in the organization of our brain. I will explore the evolution and structure of this system in Chapter 5.

Feedback and Now

Feedback, an essential part of every CAS, completes the loop of perception, circling back to the source of the transaction at the boundary. It begins our introduction to the implications of sensation and perception. Electronic systems use feedback to improve performance. There is feedback from registration back to the site of the sensation for the same reason. There is confirmation and adjustment.

We see evidence of feedback in the experience of patients recovering from trauma. Following physical trauma, people may still experience 'sensations' in parts of their bodies that no longer exist. These sensations cannot originate with actual disturbances. The modality cannot originate with a transaction location because the location is no longer there. So the disturbance must be a virtual disturbance. Cerebral systems that subsume the original feedback loops of physical sites that no longer exist stimulate these residual feedback loops and, thereby, give rise to what seem like sensations.

This cerebral interaction and feedback in a centralized, multi-modal system has important implications. While feedback may be familiar to scientists, within ourselves it presents an unexpected, totally unappreciated phenomenon... the present. No—not *a* present, but *the* present, another facet of the weirdness created by CASs. Let's go through this a step at a time.

First, there is a delay caused by the interactions and collaborations involved in the sensing of the original disturbance, its registration and its subsequent confirmation or feedback. The registration of the disturbance follows the disturbance itself by a discrete interval of time. The delay is compounded by any feedback to the site of the disturbance for confirmation and by collaborations among modalities that have different physical and cerebral boundaries, e.g. sight and touch.

Consider the distance between transistors on a chip. The distance is a limiting factor in the speed of the processor. The further the transistors are from one another, the longer they take to communicate. The body is not exempt from these laws of physics. The lapse of time is a profound, consequential aspect of this interaction.

Second, we do not detect the delay. To us, the disturbance and our registration of it happen together in real time. The anticipated outcome and the outcome are one, in the body's time. We experience the delay as the present—our own special present, an interval of time created by our nervous system.

When you hit your thumb with a hammer, it hurts immediately. Even though there is a delay as your systems interact, you don't sit there waiting for the pain. It hurts within the body-based interval of time created by your systems' interaction.

There is a conundrum here. The 'present' of science is that boundary between the past and the future. Not so with our neural systems. The systems of perception have their own present. Our lives move smoothly from one moment to the next. We don't experience delays while our systems interact—we don't detect delays as our sight collaborates with our sense of smell to identify a red rose. Nor do we hesitate while our sight and hearing collaborate to identify the direction of a threat. We experience these delays as the present... in the flow of our time. The consequential delays of feedback are our personal 'now.' It is *our* subjective present. It is where you and I live. Now.

Third, as neural registrations collaborate, they register an integrated condition of the organism—the bloodied, pulsating thumb as part of a greater whole. I call this the body state. All of the elements of the body are in some condition when the thumb is smashed—the position of your body, what all of your senses are registering, even the expletives forming but as yet unexpressed. Systems monitoring the internal condition of the body at the time also participate in the nervous system's reorganizations. Heart rate, breathing, perhaps the discomfort of a hangover, or simply distracting memories leading to the poor aim of the hammer—all make up the residual patterns reorganized after the event. Whatever residual pattern results, it is of a physical state in time of the entire nervous system. Conditions of the body's systems at the time are part of the registrations, providing a kind of 'time stamp' as part of the experience—a registration in time—your time. "Yes, I remember when..."

Subjects and Disturbance, Me and Not Me

"Hey! Stop that! Leave me alone!" How often do we hear the defense of me, the defense of my boundaries?

This whole idea of a 'me' and a 'not me' is one which science has tussled with for centuries. After all, an interpretation that is individual to an organism is subjective to that organism. It is not objective. And since science strives for objectivity, the subjective is in some manner diminished—or too often just ignored. But that's not always satisfactory, particularly when we are examining a phenomenon that is inherently subjective—the mind.

Boundaries define a self-centeredness—a system distinct from the environment. Four billion years ago, nothing had been seen, heard, or experienced—by anything else. Before there could be either a registered event or subjective feeling, there had to be something around to observe it as distinct. The properties of what existed had yet to be presented to a perceiver. This sounds like the ultimate 'can you top this?' of the tree falling in the forest, but it is an important starting point. Before there could be the registration of an event, there had to be a defined, coherent system capable of making that registration. Such a defined system must be able to demarcate itself from the event—the system must have boundaries of coherence.

What happens at the boundary is a disturbance of 'something.' On this side of the boundary, there is a distinct 'me.' On the other side is 'not me.' This simple distinction opened new adjacent possibilities for exploration by CASs. To identify what *could happen* at the boundary because of what is on the other side of the boundary is an advantage. 'Not me' became important.

Even though perceptions are limited to the modalities of sensations, from this information they recognize the pattern of what is going on out there—that is to say, the significance to 'me' of the disturbance in the outside world in the context of my experience—my initial conditions. Some of our perceptions are supported by sensing systems that operate at quite a distance from 'me.' Sight is that sense operating most remotely and able to correlate what is happening to me with what has happened out there—in 'not me.' Over time, these systems self-organized into a division of labor: one for what is happening to me and one for what is happening to 'not me'! This notion of 'otherness' led to two distinct types of neural patterns in the central system. These two systems operate in parallel; research indicates they are essentially non-overlapping systems. Both interpret the meaning of an environmental stimulus at the boundary of the body—each with very different kinds of evaluation provoked by the same stimulus. In short, sensation is about what is happening to me. Perception is about what is happening out there, *in the context of what is happening to me.*

Sight best demonstrates this partnership. The sensation of sight is lost in the overwhelming intensity of perception. When did you last sense a photon interact with your retina? Nevertheless, when the sensing systems underlying sight malfunction, the errors result in distortions. Straight lines may be slightly curved or blurred. We correct these malfunctions—errors of sensation—with contact lenses or glasses. Whereas errors of perception register errors in what is actually happening out there. Errors of perception can be disastrous. Registering a misshapen predator is one thing. Registering a friend instead of a predator is quite another! Yet, both—sensation and perception—reinforce 'me' and 'not me.'

A means for detecting and correcting errors of perception would be essential for survival. Feedback correlates perception with the original sensation as a means of error detection and correction. When the two do not quite agree, research indicates there is a bias in favor of the perceptual system. I will return to this in subsequent chapters. For now, consider the implications of 'me' and 'not me.'

While discussing 'me' I will often use 'self.' I use the word 'self' in the philosophical sense. Throughout the book, when discussing the plural of 'self,' I will use 'selfs' in order to avoid confusion with the meaning of the more common 'selves.'

Subjective-ness

Boundaries, modalities, residual patterns and feedback contribute to the distinctions between 'me' and 'not me.' Together they define a focus, a unity to which they belong, a reference within and from which they interact with 'not me.' Interactions with 'not me' are with respect to this subject of the collaborating whole. The separation of 'me' from 'not me' and the collaboration provides a dynamic, subjective reference for subsequent events: me. Within 'me,' there is that which I am, and that which I have registered—the residual patterns of my experience.

The independence of these registrations and their collaboration has another dimension. Together, these registrations comprise a focus of experience that is a point of reference. Whatever is experienced by 'me' is subject to the interpretation, the residual patterns of the previous experience of 'me.' This shared reference, the accumulation of residual patterns of dynamic self-organizations following stimulation, is unique to the set of disturbances to which the systems have been exposed. Let us call this self-referencing of registration 'the subjective realm' and let us call the experience of these collaborative systems as reflected in the residual patterns of experience, 'the self.' This experience of the self, the current state of residual neural patterns, is the essence from which any new self-organization must proceed: it is a set of initial conditions. The experience of the self influences all new perceptions.

Equally important, the coming together of this independent, distinct perception and the feedback to the origin of the disturbance opened the door to another path of adjacent possibilities. The separation of 'me' from 'not me' provides a reference for the registration of all that is happening in the environment... having meaning to me. There is a subject to which things happen. The patterns that register in me what is happening out there, are in the context of my residual patterns. They belong to me. They are my experiences of what is happening out there. These experiences are the basis for meaning to me. The patterns registered are part of the subjective-ness of me. This is essential to all aspects of me—from my feelings to my thoughts. This sense of a distinct body for reference is important to the use of metaphor and the power of metaphorical thinking grounded in our experience with the world around us. Things happen with respect to me... or not.

Yet, whatever residual patterns exist within me, whatever references are established, whatever experiences have been lived—disturbances by and in the environment write them all. Stimulation and disturbance provoke self-reorganization. But, as we will see, the stimulating environment need not be 'not me,' it need not be on the other side of the boundary that is 'me.' The environment within me is quite capable of provoking reorganization all by itself.

Once the organism and the environment—'me' and 'not me'—began self-organizing together, a completely new direction of adjacent possibilities began to appear across the evolutionary landscape. Perhaps the most dramatic was the transformation by plant life of the methane atmosphere, which characterized Earth's first three billion years, into the oxygen-oriented environment of today. Epochs ago, organisms began creating the methane suitable for their world. For 80% of its existence, Earth housed largely methane-oriented life. Then plants began to emerge. They used the carbon in the atmosphere and created the oxygen on which animal life depends. But methane life found a new home in the soil—away from the oxygen of the atmosphere. Now, ironically, man is creating an atmosphere of carbon and methane—good for plants but not too good for animals. In a process whose time span we can more easily understand, beavers build dams to create ponds in which to build their lodges. Dynamic adaptation and manipulation of the environment became possible for 'me,' too.

But not all disturbances are beyond the boundary that defines 'me.'

CASs self-organize with whatever elements are available—including elements of their own creation... their own residual patterns within me. The composite systems of the nervous system have their own boundaries and provide adjacent possibilities for the systems themselves to create 'me' and 'not me' within them.

Imaging: Perception without Sensation

The consequences of CASs incessantly self-organizing, living on the edge between stability and chaos, forming hierarchies, and seeking adjacent possibilities cannot be over-emphasized, even though you may be growing weary of it. When these systems centralized they moved into adjacent possibilities, self-organizations that did not necessarily require external stimulation. Residual patterns and restless feedback provided adjacent possibilities of self-stimulation. The centralized, multi-modal system became a rich nursery for further self-organizing without the stimulation of 'not me'. The connections and potential interactions among the centralized systems of perception multiplied. New CASs comprised of the residual patterns of multi-modal perceptions self-organized, developing their own boundaries and their own feedback. Then the inner boundaries of these CASs—the beginning and end of whole systems of sensing and perceiving—became surrogates for physical boundaries, complete with all of the processes of the physical ones. CASs are the environments of their neighbors. The surrogate boundaries of within began to assert their independence. 'Me' was able to operate without 'not me'. Imagination was born.

Consider the implications. While all the essentials of modality-based perception continue, communications also flow within other parts of the central nervous system—crossing cerebral 'surrogate surfaces' within the brain—the boundaries of cerebral systems. These surrogate sites respond to disturbances created by one another without reference back to physical boundaries. Cerebral perception was born!

What is cerebral perception? Every time you daydream... every time you imagine an event, an activity, or a relationship... there is cerebral perception at work. Cerebral perceptions do not have a body-based reference, a physical here and now. They may give rise to responses such as anxiety or pleasure. They may involve 'times' and 'places' of their own creation. They are neural patterns of what has happened, or could happen, to me or out there—self-organizing with residual patterns of actual experience. We characterize these self-organizing patterns as 'imagined.'

These imagined patterns arising in the perceptual centers of the brain cause curious anomalies. When a system of perception is busy generating images of its own, it is temporarily disengaged from perception arising out of the senses. Nevertheless, it is difficult to focus on an imagined object in the presence of a real one. Take the retina, for example. Since the imagined pattern does not match the actual sensation at the retina, we tend to reject it. The image of the real object tends to prevail. Conversely, we do not see the real object if the imagined one prevails. The system, trying to confirm the disturbance at the boundary, must choose between the physical and the cerebral boundaries. The system must choose between feedback alternatives. If we close our eyes, it is easier to imagine an object than if our eyes are open. This reduces the contention between the two overlapping systems. If light from a real object stimulates the retina while perception is focusing on an imagined object, we do not perceive the real one because the perception system is doing something else—daydreaming! The visual cortex, an important element of sight, participates in internally generated 'images.' Clinical research indicates that damage to the visual cortex causes deficiencies in imagined perceptions, too. The imagination suffers.

Ownership

"It's MINE!" the toddler screams. The awakening has begun. It is here, with our senses, that we first encounter the issue of 'ownership' in the body. My senses are incontrovertibly mine. My senses are inextricably bound to my body. They are body-based. Remember that smashed thumb? Ask your neighbor how you thumb felt. You may get empathy, but not knowledge. How do we establish that parts of our bodies are in fact ours?

The two aspects of interaction I have described—transactions and registrations—have significantly different implications for our story. First, let's look at the characteristics of sensation—transactions—as distinct from perception—registrations. Sensations belong to the organism. To the body. What is happening to me is what is happening to my body-based self. In important respects, this 'me' is isolated from everything else in the world—'me' is within the boundary of my body. Without my body, there are no sensations. Therefore, I cannot characterize what is happening to me without referring to the essence which is 'me'. My body is an integral part of my sensations. This is not necessarily true of perceptions.

The characterization of a sensation must include where it is, in or on 'my' body. Consider the consequences of your hitting your thumb. When you move your hand away from the hammer, the impression remains with you. It moves wherever you go. Perceptions don't have this same allegiance.

Sensations are always related to the kind of thing that is happening to 'me': heat, light, pressure, sound, smell. Sensations have co-evolved with the environment. If a sensation had a different quality or mode to it, it would be a different sensation. This modality-specific characteristic contrasts with perceptions. Perceptions are not concerned with the type or nature of a stimulus to 'me'. Even though perceptions have the modality of the sensation through which they obtain their information, they derive from that sensation broader information about what is going on out there— they register what is being signified about the external world.

Sensations are present-tense. Your thumb does not hurt yesterday. It hurts now. Whereas, perceptions can be of the present, or of the past—or even of the future.

The very essence of awareness is neural activity in which patterns of interaction register something happening to 'me,' at this time—whether internally or externally provoked. This self-organization begins at conception and continues through life. When an infant enters the world, she discovers the physical extent and limits of her own body by experiment. We have all watched infants play with their hands and feet—focusing on them for hours.

As our systems mature with experience, this state of sensory awareness becomes the basis for categorizing what is happening. What happens, happens with respect to my body—and nothing happens without my body, at least, so it seems when we are young. Without my body, there are no sensations, no experiences, no self-organizations, and no neuronal patterns. Without the 'me' of the infant there is no world, nothing.

'Me' does not always end at the boundary of the organism—at least not the human organism. "It's mine," the lament of the two-year-old, as she encounters more and more of the environment that is 'not me,' is only the surface of our extended engagement with the environment, an interaction in which we have vastly extended aspects of our boundaries and ourselves. I will return to this extension after we build a basis for exploring it in more depth. Now we turn to a system of particular interest to this story. Metaphor.

Suggested Additional Reading for Chapter 2

Nicholas Humphrey provides an extensive discussion of sensing and perception, and the distinctions inherent in 'me' and 'not me' in *A History of the Mind: Evolution and the Birth of Consciousness*, including the implications we highlight here. Humberto Maturana's and Francisco Varela's essay *Autopoiesis: the Organization of the Living,* in their book *Autopoiesis and Cognition: The Realization of the Living,* explores the subjective basis for 'me.' Annette Karmiloff-Smith's *Beyond Modularity: A Developmental Perspective on Cognitive Science* is suggestive of cognitive domains self-organizing in response to environmental disturbances at the boundaries defining me. Daniel Dennett in *Consciousness Explained* discusses the relationship of boundaries to the 'self.'

James Paul Gee, in *What Video Games Have to Teach Us About Learning and Literacy*, explores the relationship of patterns, pattern recognition, and experience, to learning.

Stuart Kauffman's *At Home in the Universe* explores a biological perspective of boundaries, while Humberto Maturana and Francisco Varela, in *The Tree Of Knowledge*, define the meaning of boundaries in living organisms.

CHAPTER 3
Metaphors We Live by: Emotions

This chapter explores the most primitive level of an organism's interaction with the environment—a threshold of perception and response: emotion.

So what do we mean by emotion? We are not interested in the outbursts of anger or the euphoria of love. Well, not exactly. Antonio Damasio describes emotion as a combination of a mental evaluation with dispositional bodily responses. These responses are so integrated with the perception that they are triggered without deliberation. Emotions are perceptions with pre-wired responses, changes in body states. Flushing of the skin; increased heart rate; increased attention, or alertness; rapidity or slowing of breathing; muscle tensing—all are the body's response in emotions. These body responses prepare the body for action… or not!

Why are emotions of interest to the future of the mind? We explore emotions for three reasons:

1. The primitive neural systems of emotions are the initial conditions for all other self-organizations in the brain's development; all adjacent possibilities open from them and with them.

2. They demonstrate the continuing influence of primitive initial conditions in our brain today.

3. They are the precursors of metaphor, a special case of pattern recognition of importance to mind and to this story.

Let's go back to changes in body states. I was snorkeling over the Great Barrier Reef off the coast of Fitzroy Island, Australia. It was low tide and the coral was bare inches beneath me. There were incredibly shocking colors in convoluted graceful shapes and configurations of all kinds. I was enthralled. Suddenly the hair on the back of my neck stood up. I was unable to breathe, to kick or move my arms. I turned icy cold in the warm water, drifting powerlessly. What was going on? Then my rational mind caught up and began to tell me things. There, almost face-to-face with me, no more than six inches beneath me, was what seemed like a gaping mouth—twelve inches across. The openness was dark, velvety, and pulsating... alive! My rational mind recognized it as a huge clam. Did my rational mind help? No. My body and brain were still under the control of the limbic system nestled around my brain stem. It found memories, residual patterns that fit the circumstances. Were they of some B movie I had seen as a child—a pearl diver in the clasp of a giant clam struggling to surface for air? Or was it more primitive? I was barely able to move my flippers—the opening was now inches below my stomach. Slowly, my reason returned. But my snorkeling was ruined for the day. Reason didn't matter. I knew better than to be frightened, but my emotions were not about to release me from override. Not that quickly.

The first imperative of the brain is to manage the body's survival. These imperatives are fundamental initial conditions of that most formidable CAS, the brain. Since the emotional systems emerged early in the history of the brain, they are a foundation for the systems emerging after them. Outside of our awareness, they subtly penetrate and interact with all of the systems in the brain and the body. Clinical research shows that humans deprived of their emotional systems do not make rational decisions.

Damasio believes that we rely not only on the limbic system but on parts of the prefrontal cortex, and those brain sectors that 'map and integrate signals from the body.' A feeling is a view, at a moment in time, of the state of the body and of specific neural systems which support it and which integrate signals related to bodily structure and regulation, and which our most refined thoughts and best actions, accomplishments and emotions, use as a yardstick.

In life we seldom encounter identical environmental circumstances, identical residual patterns of experience. The systems responsible for protecting us register key characteristics of the new circumstance in the context of residual patterns having similar characteristics. Environmental circumstances may differ. Details may differ. The new experience is registered in the context of the old, residual, patterns.

What does this have to do with metaphor?

Lakoff and Johnson tell us that metaphor is understanding and experiencing one kind of thing in terms of another. That description could apply to emotion, too.

There are some aspects of emotion we should explore before taking up metaphor.

Be Quick… or be Dead

Emotions prepare the body for immediate action. Emotions are not deliberative. Who has not felt the rush of adrenalin in the face of a challenge, whether physical or mental, real or imagined? Meanwhile reactions—drives and instincts, lurking in the neural patterns—generate behavior with the preparation of emotions. Drives and instincts are bodily manifestations of emotions.

Our sensing of disturbances in the environment triggers emotions. As we have seen, our experience of different sensations and perceptions is registered in the form of residual patterns of self-organization caused by the original stimulation. Our reactions and responses that occur as a result of this stimulation take the form of new self-organizing patterns—moving into possibilities adjacent to each successive residual pattern, each successive experience. These become the initial conditions for the next experience, the next stimulation. They self-organize starting from these initial conditions and end in a pattern that is adjacent to the beginning pattern. New stimuli resonating with residual patterns of experience, or predispositions acquired through eons of passing through adjacent possibilities, set responses in motion. Emotions respond with un-deliberative preparation. They respond quickly.

In the course of our evolution, separate functional neural systems self-organized in order to respond to different classes of circumstances. Each has different triggers and distinct systems for responding. Each then generates behavior unique to the circumstances—for the good of the organism. The triggers and the response evolved together—on the same evolutionary landscape. Each participated in self-organizations through the adjacent possibilities of the other.

Emotions are the body's preparation for action and the interconnection of the emotional systems with the neocortex admits emotion into the seat of reason.

While different species may respond in different modes—eat, fight or flight—they indicate that the emotions appeared far back in the sequence of adjacent possibilities. The evaluation function of emotions is strange to us rational animals. The processing is non-conscious. The speed is unthinking, sometimes uncomfortable. Yet, emotions persist in our actions and thoughts today. They were the initial conditions for our survival and are now the initial conditions for our present.

Close Enough is Good Enough

Emotions are tuned to high level 'whole' circumstances that may include a multitude of factors that are dissimilar in detail once analyzed, but share prominent characteristics. The circumstances that evoke a particular set of emotional responses may even constitute entirely different contexts.

Emotions are not discriminating. If it is close enough, prepare! Better to prepare for action in error than to be eaten in error. Emotions improve our chances of survival: they prepare the body for action.

Emotions are the metaphors of biology. Metaphor enables us to understand one kind of thing in terms of another—even if seemingly different in total. Similarly, emotions enable us to 'understand' one thing in the context of another. Emotions enable us to prepare for response to a new thing in the context of experiences of the past. Emotions prepare us to react to disturbances or circumstances that are similar to those that make up our residual patterns, but not necessarily exact reproductions.

The evaluations of emotion are the earliest metaphors. The residual patterns of these systems open adjacent possibilities for new self-organizations; preparation for disturbances having only partial similarity to the residual patterns of the past. The emergence of metaphor in pattern recognition is a basis for cognition.

The Circuitry of Emotions

However much we may intellectualize the brain, its basic purpose is to ensure the survival of the body. As we explore higher order functions such as intellectual, personal, and social activities, we should not forget that they are intimately interconnected with these original initial conditions. Systems critical to survival reside in the limbic system, particularly the amygdala, the hypothalamus, and the hippocampus. Self-organizations in this old brain are both predisposed and learned. Still other systems embellish these systems of the old brain, participating in the mobilizations and dispositions of the body's emotions and feelings.

Nested reactions affect innumerable local and global systems throughout the body in the interest of survival—that most important of long-since initial conditions. These initial conditions perpetuate the priority of survival through extensive interconnection with systems underlying the higher functions of the cortex—to the occasional disruption of those higher functions.

Emotions operate in two modes: slow and fast. The latter are supported by 'direct connections,' the expressways of survival. They bypass deliberation and consideration. The circuits of emotion also include chemical messengers loosed in the blood stream, altering the function of cells in remote systems. The cortex is not exempt from either influence.

When self-organizing residual patterns in the old brain are inconclusive, these patterns collaborate with the cortex for enriched pattern recognition. Hormones are main-lined. There is heightened activity in collaborating brain areas alerting the sensory systems, focusing on the stimulus for more thorough pattern registration, enabling more extensive pattern recognition. The cortex, once commandeered by the emotions, drops all else and responds for survival. It is red alert. The cortex is overwhelmed with nature's double espresso.

The responses of the emotions are pervasive. They include every system of the body: hormonal, cardiovascular, musculature, even blood vessels in the skin. All systems collaborate in preparing to support survival of the whole—before you 'know' it. Knowledge of, and regulation of, the body is necessary. These patterns reside in multiple regions of the brain. This seemingly haphazard diaspora is the consequence of wandering through adjacent possibilities. Changes in the brain have taken place in local, functional sub-systems, their connections, and their interactions. Increases in resources have satisfied functional needs. The totality of the brain and its emotions are the consequence of these multiple self-organizations through adjacent possibilities.

Quick Time… and Slow Time Too

How many of us have felt foolish after these emotions precipitate an uncalled-for response? The pervasive interconnection of the neural systems underlying emotion with 'higher' levels of the brain is an awkward relationship.

The principal purpose of the brain remains quick response for survival. Yet, these defensive systems influence attention and memory. They intervene in processes affecting perception, learning, recall, reasoning, and creativity. Emotion influences that 'gut-feeling' experienced when encountering a long lost love, or the competitor who cheated you. The compelled collaboration of the cortex contributes a wide range of slower responses and a more comprehensive evaluation based on experience.

This collaboration with the cortex has opened up opportunities for more nuanced responses to stimuli. Emotions are sometimes modulated by the sophistication of moderation, deliberation, or the persistent duration of a threat. We characterize this condition as moods, those 'up days' and the 'downers.' Nevertheless, no matter how many triggers are learned, no matter how many subtleties we employ, there is a limited number of responses.

There are three implications of this collaboration with the cortex:

1. The cortex introduces more response alternatives, and gives us the capability to register new experiences and mediate primitive ones. It enhances interactions with the stimuli of sophisticated, augmenting environments such as the Internet. The many connections between the limbic system and the neocortex also make it possible for the neocortex to arouse emotions. Have you ever wanted to throttle a blogger? Our visceral reactions to on-line provocations do not really differ from those that are face-to-face. We simply have more time to control them.

2. This collaboration gives rise to longer-term dispositions for response—moods and personalities. Thought processes can be slowed or accelerated, recalled images can proliferate, or decrease, novel combinations of residual patterns can be created, enhanced, or halted. Learned social conventions and ethics can shape instinctual behavior, making it flexible and adaptive in complex environments.

3. The collaborative residual registrations of emotion and cognition are owned experiences—memories. However, not all aspects of an event are remembered equally well—memories can be selective and incomplete. Memories are reconstructions—they are not necessarily accurate in all detail. Memories important to survival are rich in the specific characteristics that will trigger the emotions. It is this incomplete, inaccurate memory that can cause us embarrassment in the complicated world of today. It is also another opening into the adjacent possibilities of metaphor.

How are You Feeling?

What about those subjective states, the feelings that accompany emotion? Feelings have their origin in the longer term influence of emotion. While emotions affect the body state—a rush of adrenalin or flushing of the skin, feelings are the perception of that body state. Feelings are the slower to arise perception of what is happening to me as a consequence of emotion. That rush of adrenalin may manifest itself in 'feelings' of fear, or anger, or lust! These feelings come from registrations of our body state collaborating with other systems in the brain. Our systems of pattern recognition and evaluation may differ from stimulus to stimulus, from event to event, not because the systems evaluating are different, but because the systems collaborating with our body states are different—providing different input for evaluation. Feelings arise from the collaboration of systems of survival with more sophisticated systems of evaluation. Why are emotional events perceived differently than unemotional ones? Feelings arise after emotions. Emotions prepare our body for encounters with a disturbance. Muscles may be tensed or relaxed. Blood pressure may be increased or lowered. Chemical messengers are loosed throughout the body in the blood stream. Pupils may dilate. The alarms are sounded. The body is on full alert. The systems regulating the body register these changes. They know something is amiss.

Feelings modify our perceptions by juxtaposing patterns of the body's state at the time of disturbance with residual patterns of the body's undisturbed state, perhaps body state when adrenalin is not rushing through our body. Feelings have an inextricable connection to the body. I feel, therefore I am.

More sophisticated evaluations emerge from patterns that include the primitive initial conditions, the residual patterns of emotion, and the more deliberative systems of the neocortex. Self-organizations of the present can only spring from the residual patterns, the initial conditions of the past. The essence of feeling is the perception of the state of the body. Feelings occur in the province of the five senses. There are no non-sensory feelings.

Feelings may be predisposed or acquired through experience. These patterns develop early, continuing as initial conditions for life—a reference for whatever follows. Feelings alter how we perceive the world and ourselves—and how we think. That is an inescapable consequence of our primitive initial conditions.

Thinking, Feelings and Interactions

"It was written all over your face!" How often have we heard that? Humans have a range of facial expressions for communicating that is unique. Infants can discriminate between faces at birth, prefer familiar ones after a few days, and use facial expressions after a month. These facial expressions project feelings associated with their responses to stimuli—they reflect emotions. This means of communication is very important for the pre-verbal period of infants—a not so subtle, and persistent sequence of initial conditions.

In more deliberative responses, innate patterns of emotion can incline responses away from or toward alternatives, short-cutting many evaluations and hastening decisions. Emotions preclude the evaluation of every alternative, reducing our choices and making response-time practical in the real world. That is a survival advantage that machines do not have. Humans deprived of emotional systems become indecisive or make irrational decisions. The relationship between emotions and rational behavior is part of the biological machinery of survival... and of thinking.

Thinking with emotion? Isn't that an oxymoron? What we characterize as thinking depends on the handmaid of memory. Memory—long, short, working, wired or learned—is associated with neural systems collaborating with the limbic system; with the hippocampus. The hippocampus invigorates all the neurons collaborating in an experience-specific self-organization. So are we saying that memory is emotional? In a sense, yes. But for now we simply observe that in the case of the limbic system, it is not who you are, it is who you know. The limbic system is well connected. We will explore this important relationship when we consider the brain.

Self-organizations following a stimulus take place throughout the interconnected neural systems. The residuals are a unique pattern differing from the initial conditions. This subjective pattern includes both emotional and body-state monitoring systems. The participation of the limbic system activates other systems we attribute to emotional response. These responses reinforce all self-reorganizations active at the time of the collaboration. Just as the body marks time, the body marks memory, and memory is essential to survival and thinking. This relationship will become clear when we explore the systems of the brain.

It seems perverse to ascribe only emotion and the regulation of the body's life and survival functions to the limbic system if it is active in a cognitive function like memory. It seems equally perverse to insist on the separation of emotion and thinking. The limbic system participates in key elements of thinking. These primitive initial conditions of survival persist in the residual conditions, the residual patterns of our systems of today. The systems preparing the body for action in the interests of survival are with us today. We should expect these systems to collaborate in the self-organizations of the brain today—including those reaching beyond survival. They are the metaphors… the patterns we live by. Emotions—preparation for action—will influence the future of the mind in ways we may not expect.

Before we explore the limbic system and the brain we will consider the systems of sight. Sight not only underlies the trajectory of vision, it also allows us to sneak up on the complexity of the brain.

Suggested Additional Reading for Chapter 3

Antonio Damasio has a series of books exploring the neural systems underlying emotion and reason, and their inextricable collaboration. Particularly helpful are *Descartes' Error: Emotion, Reason and The Human Brain*, and *The Feeling of What Happens: Body and Emotion in the Making of Consciousness*. Daniel Goleman's *Emotional Intelligence* further explores emotion's pre-emptive role and Joseph LeDoux explores the importance of consciousness to feelings in *The Emotional Brain*.

George Lakoff and Mark Johnson, in *Metaphors We Live By*, explore the structure of metaphor as concept, activity, and language—a good start for our exploration of metaphor and cognition.

CHAPTER 4
Sight

Why do I introduce sight? Why not vision? Vision is one of the three trajectories of the future of the mind. I draw a distinction between sight and vision. As we will see later, vision gets a lot of help from systems throughout the nervous system other than sight. Vision is not simply sight.

Sight is important to our story for several reasons. Sight:

- is the legacy of a set of systems with which early life began and a principal set from which vision emerges.

- registers remote objects before contact, before threats are threatening.

- is a small, approachable piece of the brain itself—sticking out so to speak, giving us an opportunity to sneak up on the enormous complexity of the brain.

- is a marvelous system for illustrating how CASs can encompass disparate elements from physics, chemistry, and biology into a single, sub-optimal, yet working system.

Exploring sight before plunging into vision also serves to distinguish between the two and prepares us for important distinctions later.

In the latter parts of the book we will explore how the future of the mind will emerge from systems of biology, electronics and software. Exploring the diverse domains contributing sight will prepare us for that.

I am going to approach this subject in three ways:

1. We will do a fly-over to get the big picture of the major physical systems of sight and their general relationships to one another.

2. We will explore some of the details that define the building blocks of the nervous system and sight.

3.   We will look at how these systems and their relationships might have developed over time, moving through a series of adjacent possibilities. When we finish with this, you may wonder how in the world you see. Yet, it will aid in our exploration of the future of the mind.

It should be noted at the start that, unlike many CASs, the sub-systems of sight are of little value independent of the whole. All are needed to effect sight.

The View from 35,000 Feet

The systems of sight interact with almost non-existent particles in the environment: photons. There are gazillions of photons ricocheting off everything. These bundles of energy travel as waves with specific frequencies of variation. As waves, they are light. As interactions with our systems of sight, they are particles. And according to quantum physics, we won't know which they are until we interact with them. This is not an encouraging beginning.

The eye dynamically prepares for interaction with the environment more than any other sense organ.

- The aperture responds to the photon monsoons and droughts of brightness and darkness, opening and closing, controlling the number of photons entering the eye—not too many and not too few, but just right!

- The cornea or lens controls the path of light through the eye. A whole package of musculature sub-systems, in response to commands from the brain, open and close the aperture and flex and bend this convex lens just enough to bring about the sweet spot necessary for focusing photons from the source of interest on to the retina. Focusing requires exquisite feedback and collaboration between the optic systems of the eye and the supporting muscular systems.

- The vitreous is a clear substance that maintains the structural integrity of the eye, and digests the detritus sloughed off by the living cells of the eye—floaters.

All three optimize the path of photons for interaction with the retina. Thanks to this preparation, the eye captures photons in a range of circumstances, across a spectrum of wavelengths: from bright sunlight to dark clouded nights; in the dim light of caves; distinguishing shaded objects in a glaring background, both near and far. This preparation is in the realm of biology.

Photons passing through these elements strike the photoreceptors in the retina. The energy conversion takes place here in a combination of quantum physics and chemistry. The light wave becomes a particle in the interaction and a chemical reaction in the photoreceptors depends on the ebb and flow of dye-like pigment that absorbs the particle energy of photons in the frequencies of visible light.

The photoreceptors are of two types: rods capture dim light while cones capture bright light and color. Special cones in the center of the eye differentiate precisely among the incoming paths of many closely flying photons providing fine resolution where we focus our attention. There are three types of cone cell responding to photons with specific energies—red, blue, and green.

Pattern recognition begins in the retina. The photoreceptors are directly connected to other cells in the retina that react to different levels of photon intensity. Different shapes cast different photon patterns on the retina.

The spherical working surface of our eye is like a curved IMAX movie screen. This improves the detection of the sources of photons projected by the edges of the environment. This curvature enables the retina to capture photons entering the aperture from almost 180 degrees in all directions, instead of only those photons coming in a straight line at the small aperture. It is the difference between seeing a point in front of you, and taking in the entire landscape. The result is a relationship between the shape of the source of the photons and the interactions with the arrays of photoreceptors. For example, a stick stimulates a straight line pattern; a ball stimulates a filled circle. These patterns are not to be confused with images.

The most effective use of this photon capturing system would be to monitor which transaction clusters are capturing photons, when, how many and from which angles. Each improvement in evaluation would provide a marginally improved capability for surviving. This evaluative capability is in the visual cortex, at the back of the head.

The visual cortex is the centralized area for registration in the perceptual system of sight. The visual cortex is also referred to as the occipital lobes.

The visual cortex demonstrates the power of networks self-organizing into hierarchies of systems. Some attention to the subject of hierarchies here will aid our understanding of cyberous augmentation and collaboration in the future of the mind. There is a hierarchy of neuronal systems in the visual cortex. Each of the hierarchical areas adds its own bit of refinement to the information obtained with the eyes' transactions .

Within the visual cortex, in each of 5 levels, there are nuclei of neurons—neighborhoods of neurons that have close relationships, groups that spend time talking among themselves—interacting and collaborating toward some conclusion or output. This output is then available at the next level of collaborating neurons—at another level of processing where the consequences of the lower level are available as elements for self-organization.

As information ascends to higher levels of neuronal systems in the visual cortex, there is increasing abstraction of the visual pattern in the neurons and more collaboration with other systems of the brain. Registrations of interactions through other senses collaborate and the body's monitoring systems contribute subjective time and conditions. The residuals of past impressions contribute continuity.

What exactly is going on here? Each collaborative neighborhood of neurons—each internal debate resulting in some effect—has an output, which is then available for use as a basic element in another, higher order CAS. A new property of registration emerges that is then available for the next level in the hierarchy. This is nothing more or less than a hierarchy of CASs, each using the set of CASs below as the basic elements for the next level of self-organization leading to the next emergent property.

Ganglions connect the front to the back. They keep the eye in touch with the rest of the brain. They are long neurons that reach from the retina to the visual cortex in the back of the head. Collectively, they constitute the optic nerve.

Some Defining Aspects of Sight

The objective here is not to become an expert on the neurobiology of the systems of sight. Rather, the objective is to achieve a better understanding of the breadth and depth of the complex adaptive systems comprising sight, to begin understanding the elemental building blocks of the brain itself, and to prepare for exploring the brain's augmentation and collaboration with the environment for the emergence of the future of the mind.

What happens after the energy of the photon is captured is truly marvelous, and more germane to our story. Both the retinal neurons and the ganglia engage in editing before the visual cortex even learns of the transaction. Each provides a basis for adding to the experience registered in the residual patterns of the systems of sight. The retinal neurons, amacrines, also deserve special attention.

The retina is an amazing balance of chaos and structure—of priorities and functions—and quantum physics—of energy absorption of photo-cellular reaction and chemistry. It is comprised of neuronal systems with connections reaching to other parts of the brain. It has a blood barrier similar to the brain's protecting it from meddlesome substances. As in the brain, special cells, here called glial cells, fill the space between the neurons of the retina. Early in the development of the embryo, the retina derives from the same neural tube as the brain. The retina is not simply part of the eye; it is part of the brain, sticking out there to see what is happening.

The human retina has some 166 million photocells, each with 91 layers to absorb photons. That's over 15 billion receptors on the lookout for the errant photon. The sensitivity of these interactions is remarkable. The voltage fluctuations of photon impacts are at the quantum level. As few as *seven* receptor cells energized in a line at the retina can stimulate a response in the visual cortex. That is seven quantum events occurring across a field of over 15 billion.

The retina is an incredible agglomeration of little cells just trying to do their own thing in their own CAS—and not necessarily to help us see. There is no central director sending out orders to these cells nor to the systems of cells, telling them what to do so we can see. These are CASs self-organizing according to their own rules. Yet a surprising amount of processing takes place within the retina itself.

The photocells of the retina are interconnected with collaborative assemblies of neurons. These areas, only 1mm across, function in networks, conduct transactions in unison, share transactions with others, and share a connection to the brain. The photoreceptors may belong to more than one transaction area. The connections themselves also combine, or merge, so that not only do transactions from overlapping areas end up on different connections to the brain, the circuits themselves end up sharing reports of transactions from different areas. Any single transaction, any single photon, can affect the retina's neuronal system in numerous ways simultaneously. It seems to be a chaotic mess, but close examination discloses exquisite balance and order; truly operating at the edge of chaos. The patterns of these initial reorganizations are then elements for use in higher order CASs.

The ganglion network connects the retina with the visual cortex in the back of the brain. They also participate in the hierarchical self-organizing of sight.

The pattern of disturbance in transaction areas is important to the response of any one ganglion. Each ganglion gathers output from an area of the retina. Many receptors contribute to the response of a single ganglion. Yet, one receptor may also contribute to the response of a number of ganglia. Some react to disturbances near the center of the ganglion's area of interest, or on the edges of the areas, or to the stability of a disturbance, or to movement of a source, to the beginning of movement, or to the end of movement, or at the beginning and end of movement. Some respond as long as light is present, some as long as light is absent. As ganglia leave the transaction areas, they merge like branches on a tree leading toward the roots, amalgamating the transactions they have collected.

So, the effects of the retinal transactions reach the visual cortex only after several self-organizations along the way. Important to the future of the mind, the experience of post-birth development influences ganglion development. Initial repeated interactions in the ganglion lay down the residual states that will forever influence subsequent registrations of interaction with the environment. Kittens, raised in an environment devoid of horizontal lines, are unable as mature cats to see steps!

There is one final defining characteristic of sight that is of importance here because it biases sight... and vision, to the influence of post-birth development. Before exploring it, we need a little briefing on the fundamentals of the nervous system. This will also prepare us to explore the brain.

The neuron is the basic element of the nervous system. Neurons as elements of a CAS have exchanges among themselves. Like all cells, they must participate in the business of staying alive, but neuronal networks self-organize to exchange information from one to another and combine different kinds of information together in patterns. The registration of environmental stimuli in a network pattern is a form of information and the residual state of the self-organization is knowledge of experience with that environment. Neurons have boundaries. The most important functional parts of the neuron to us are at the boundary where neighbors share signals. There are two boundary areas of interest: dendrites and axons.

Dendrites accept inputs that influence the cell. A neuron can have numerous dendrites entering. An axon shares the excitation of the neuron with other neurons—sort of like a long finger pushing the buttons (dendrites) of other neurons. A neuron has only one axon exiting. Think of it this way: lots of dendrites in, commotion, one axon out... but with lots of branches to other dendrites. An axon connects with dendrites of other cells. A single axon may influence the dendrites of numerous other neurons. Conversely, several neurons through their branching axons may influence a single neuron simultaneously, or numerous neurons simultaneously.

These interactions take place in a synapse, where changes in electro-chemical potential take place as ions are passed back and forth. There is that slow chemical domain again. Slow? Imagine the agony of using a smartphone or a laptop that operated at the rate of a few thousands of operations each second instead of gigahertz—billions of operations each second. Yet the pokey old nervous system does get the job done.

The interactions may have varying levels of intensity, or they may be simply on/off. Neurons react to stimulation by either discharging through their axon to other neurons or inhibiting discharge. When an axon of one neuron and dendrites of others have repeated interactions, the stimulation threshold becomes more favorable—there is a bias favoring the relationship. Scientists call this the Long Term Potentiation or LTP.

Now back to defining aspects of sight. Some neurons in the retina are distinctive. They have no axons—no long fingers for pushing the buttons (dendrites) of other neurons. Axon-less neurons, amacrines, seem to include synaptic processes within their dendrites. Amacrine cells are not unique to the retina but their concentration there is unequaled. The photoreceptors connect directly to amacrine cells in the retina. A differentiating characteristic of the human nervous system is an intense, abundant structure of amacrines. So what makes them so special?

Amacrine cells specialize in talking to themselves and to their local neighbors without involving the entire neuron. And they do it quickly.

They seem to possess some means for their dendrites to both stimulate and be stimulated by themselves with no help from discharging axons. They cluster together in little neighborhoods called nuclei, about 1 mm across— little self-organizing systems. There is considerable internal, intra-dendrite chatter and direct dendrite-to-dendrite debate among those in the neighborhood cluster. This debate in the clusters leads to reinforcement or reduction of the signal impact. Why? And why is that important?

Discharges in the photo receptor cells vary relatively little over a wide range of photon stimulation. There is little distinction between events. One photon is just like another. Yet there are substantial differences when the signals enter the ganglia on the way to the visual cortex. How does this happen? If a photon energizes the center of a cluster, the amacrines on the edges of the cluster don't just sit there—they emphasize the event. They pump themselves up, so to speak, to be as different as possible in the opposite direction, to bring about a sharp distinction between the center and the edge of the group. They take this simple transaction—a photon energizing a photo receptor—and they make it into a big event in which that receptor's condition is contrasted with all of its neighbors. The very essence of pattern recognition is recognition of a difference and these amacrines intensify the differences among billions of receptors.

The point here is that the amacrines contribute something to the signal that is passed on to the visual cortex and do so without the delay of a multitude of axon/dendrite handoffs. At this very early stage in the transaction/registration process, the effect received by the visual cortex is different than the simple cause, the transaction with the photon at the retina. There is processing. Something has been added. Amacrine cells in the retina underlie complex receptive field properties such as the detection of motion, direction, and orientation.

Retinal neurons have another important distinction. As with ganglia, their development and initial self-organization occur after birth. They are the cells in the nervous system most exposed to environmental influence, to that influence propagated by culture.

So why have we dwelt on retinal neurons? First, we have noted the Long Term Potentiation, the bias developed by repeated stimulation of groups or patterns of neurons. There is a tendency to 'see' what we have seen before. Second, amacrine cells, most dense in the retina's early processing of the transactions of sight, develop after birth and are most subject to the influence of post-birth development. These two phenomena contribute to an astonishing process: vision must be learned and early learning, initial conditions, influence what is subsequently learned. We will elaborate on this in the chapter on vision.

Before that, how might sight have come about? And what does that tell us about the future of mind?

The Evolution of Sight

We don't really know how our sight evolved. Yet, exploring the possibilities, and the diverse assembly of physical laws and domains that have been accessed by the adjacent possibilities of the CAS comprising sight will prepare us to explore the diverse collaborations in the future of the mind. So what was the likely starting point?

Basic sensing and perception arose early at the boundaries of organisms. Yet, unlike some of the collaborative operations of the body we might examine, the several systems comprising the system of sight have little if any value separately. In collaboration, they comprise one of the most complex physical systems we will meet—short of the brain. How could this complex system come to be? How—in the absence of precursor collaborating systems which are holding down other jobs—how did the sense of sight come to be?

Research has shown that all species with eyes have very similar DNA responsible for producing eyes, a strong suggestion that at some point in the ancient past, life seized on photons as a means for remote sensing and never let go. The threshold development was most likely the evolution of a surface that was sensitive to a barrage of photons—to the 'touch' of sunlight. Such a capability could have provided both a source of energy and a sense of direction.

Gradual improvements would have emerged in the use of these captured photons. The registration of these boundary events was available for use by other CASs. Each incremental advantage gained would confer an additional survival advantage: marginal change could yield marginal benefit. Once begun, this remote sensing system would have likely persisted in all environments in which photons were encountered.

The nature of the photon itself must have posed a challenge. If an organism really wants to use one of these elusive little critters, the system must first concentrate on stopping and holding on to it. It follows that the more layers of capturing cells, the better. There would have been other marginal improvements in the exploration of adjacent possibilities: increased surface for photon capture, guiding the photon, direction detection, a system for evaluating the differences in the angles and intensities of photons, and cell collaboration—are just some of them.

It would have taken little for the emergence of the bowl shape to begin. Possibilities adjacent to a flat surface of photon-capturing cells would likely include surface imperfections. A slight bump or a minor depression in a surface would be rewarded by a marginal improvement and a whole series of adjacent possibilities and initial conditions would be opened up for exploration. The deeper the bowl, the better the capacity for discriminating between the different directions from which the photons are coming.

The fossil record fails us—soft tissue doesn't often fossilize. But computer simulation has shown that it could take as little as 500,000 years to evolve a bendable lens if the initial conditions are a bowl-shaped photon detector with a protective membrane. Throughout this exploration of adjacent possibilities, there would have been several stages in which the eye was quite serviceable to some living organism. We see this in the eyes of other creatures.

The collaboration of biology, physics, and chemistry in the systems of sight should not come as a surprise. All of life combines these disciplines. The processes operating at different levels within the hierarchies operate with different rules, and at different speeds. CASs do not divide elements into categories, whether they be animal, vegetable or mineral... or synthetic. CASs self-organize from the elements available in order to move into an adjacent possibility. This is a lesson to remember as we enter the realms of synthetic, cyberous augmentation in future chapters.

This collaboration we call sight, however awesome it may be, is only preparation for exploring the most awesome CAS known. The brain is our next subject.

Suggested Additional Reading for Chapter 4

Richard Dawkins, in *The Blind Watchmaker*, discusses possible alternatives for the evolution of sight, and in the process, explores the systems of sight.

Bruno Breitmeyer, in *Blindspots: The Many Ways We Cannot See*, examines the organization of the systems of sight and the hierarchies of self-organizing; the importance of early interaction with the environment; and what these systems can do, and what they cannot do.

Philip Lieberman demonstrates the importance of preconditions in *Uniquely Human*. For the curious, John Dowling's *The Retina* explores the retina in all the depth you could want.

CHAPTER 5
The Brain

Claude Monet was among those to recognize the human penchant for pattern recognition. He observed that all noses are different, but we never fail to recognize one.

This is the last chapter in our exploration of the physical components giving rise to mind. Following perception and sight, our brain is the third stop as we trace the progression of pattern recognition in the human nervous system. With approximately 10^{20} neurons having gazillions of interconnections, consuming some 20% of the body's energy, and requiring an elaborate cooling system to dissipate the heat it generates, the brain is a formidable subject. While handling seemingly routine operations that challenge the most sophisticated robots science can design, performing analyses that supercomputers struggle to match, and effecting communications in a highly sophisticated sound system that uses compression techniques only recently understood, it also recognizes all sorts of patterns beyond the capabilities of our best artificial intelligence efforts. Yet, it just pokes along at a snail's pace. We would expect an operating speed at least in the gigahertz if not picohertz range. But no, the brain cycles at a rate in the milliseconds. It is not some high speed electronic whiz-bang. It functions with the slow speed of chemical reactions.

The brain has enormous resources of self-organizing CASs, employs two quirks in the domains of complexity, and is the seat of human pattern recognition. In this chapter I will focus on the brain as organ. The mind comes later.

I will explore the major physical systems of our brain, their functions, their relationships, some of the details underlying the relationships, and consider how these systems might have moved through sequences of adjacent possibilities to form our pride and joy.

An exploration of the structure of the brain will provide insights into how CASs can occupy strange configurations as they move into a sequence of adjacent possibilities. We will also gain insight into the potential for still stranger configurations in the future.

THE FUTURE OF THE MIND

The Physical Structure of the Human Brain

Science has divided the brain into five physical parts for analysis: the brain stem, the cerebellum, the limbic system, the cerebrum, and the cerebral cortex. The brain stem, the most primitive part, formed about 500 million years ago. An enlargement at the top of the spinal cord, it controls functions such as breathing.

Wrapped around the brain stem like a sweatband is the cerebellum. It is our body's automatic pilot, managing systems for motion and balance, and 'learned' activities like walking.

The limbic system looks like a warped wishbone sitting on top of the brain stem at the base of the cerebral cortex. Complex networks of interacting systems, its interconnections with the neocortex are an essential link for consciousness, experiences, and emotions. It maintains our cool by managing body temperature, blood pressure, heart rate, and other aspects of our well-being. This is where primitive survival actions begin—the seat of emotion. Yet, it is directly wired to that part of the brain which defines us as human—the neocortex. It plays an important role in memory.

The cerebrum is a mattress for the cerebral cortex. It looks like a heavily wrinkled turban wrapped around the rest of the brain parts; connecting circuits of the cerebral cortex weave through it.

The cerebral cortex, sometimes referred to simply as the cortex, looks like a spray-painted effort to cover up design errors. Barely ⅛ inch thick, it clings to every nook and cranny of the wrinkled turban, about one square meter of surface area. It contains more neurons than the rest of the brain put together—about 10^{10} neurons. This is where the serious stuff happens. Self-organizations here are collaborations stimulated by other parts of the brain. This is where you live.

The Modularity of the Brain

My purpose in the next two sections is not to provide an in-depth understanding of the neurobiology of the brain. Rather, it is to illustrate how a sequence of initial conditions and self-organization can lead to strange configurations and seemingly sub-optimal consequences. Here we will explore a mélange of nature's mash-ups that will prepare us to consider the potential for the future of the mind. If you should become frustrated as you read ahead, consider how the brain must feel!

Modules of the cortex provide division of labor in the brain. Four pair are defined by location and general function. The frontal lobes—on the right and left behind the forehead—are where routine planning and preparation take place. The temporal lobes—behind the temples—handle hearing and memory. The parietal lobes—on top—self-organize what we sense of the outside world, making these the home base for the original 'virtual reality.' As I mentioned in Chapter 4, the visual cortex or occipital lobes at the back are devoted to sight.

The brain is also split into two hemispheres like a shelled walnut. The two are inter-connected by hundreds of millions of fibers supporting continuous communication. Why? Our brain is organized asymmetrically. The corresponding lobes in each hemisphere have different responsibilities. Nature gave us two brains for the price of one.

The lobes on the left hand side of the brain run the right side of the body and vice versa. If you move your right hand, the muscles are managed by the left side of the brain. The dominant side of the brain is also responsible for speech. The other side does the writing. The left side handles numerical analysis, while the right does the creative thinking and the synthesis of abstract concepts like music and art. Characteristics of personality reside in the right, but the ability to express that personality through speech sits in the left. While the 'person' sits on the right, the communicator sits on the left. The area responsible for speech also has some responsibility for cognition. Starting to sound like the amalgamation we found in the systems of sight?

The additional readings at the end of the chapter provide extensive discussion of the asymmetry. We need only a glimpse of the crazy-quilt division of labor to appreciate nature's penchant for self-organizing into Rube Goldberg systems that perform tasks in convoluted, unpredictable ways. Appreciating this unpredictable organization will be important when we consider the future of the mind.

Modularity or Chaos?

Let's examine the lobes in more detail and then delve into some inexplicable relationships we can only attribute to the vagaries of self-organization into adjacent possibilities.

The left frontal lobe is associated with the motor activity of language, the production of sounds, and their assembly into words. The right frontal lobe is involved in recall, particularly musical and spatial pattern recognition such as drawing and writing.

The left temporal lobe specializes in semantics of speech, mediating the verbalization, sequencing the sounds in the proper order, and the intonation and rhythm of speech. The right temporal lobe participates in the processing of visual information such as drawing, writing, spatial recognition, and spatial pattern recognition.

The left parietal lobe participates in the semantics of speech production and recognition, integrating sensory data with language, supporting gestures, the motions for writing, and enabling verbal knowledge of the body. The right parietal lobe specializes in recall relating the body to its surroundings: movement through the environment; the integration of visual inputs like writing, printing, and auditory inputs; and spatial organization tasks that require the coordination of visual cues such as map reading. It is particularly active in the perception of irregular patterns such as those required for the detection of facial features.

The occipital lobes, also referred to as the visual cortex, are devoted to sight. While smaller than those of other primates, they are more intensely and extensively interconnected with other parts of the brain.

While the modularity of the brain is explored in generally available texts, there is less discussion of the brain's further fragmented organization—an organization that could be described as chaotic.

Research has identified small, discrete areas in which neighboring—even remotely 'networked'—neurons can be identified in collaboration and 'disassociation' at various times in the execution of very specific functions. It is like members of soccer teams in a league, constantly leaving one team for another and then returning only to leave again. Normally this happens temporarily—one fragment of a neuronal system may disassociate from a task that is not in progress and collaborate on another, subsequently returning to the first... or perhaps still another. These are CASs self-organizing in response to stimuli. Disassociations can become permanent. Clinically, disassociations are revealed when a disability within the brain leads to a dysfunctional capacity in a person—an incapacity that seems to be, intuitively, incomplete and which leaves part of a function still operating. For example, in word deafness, speech is heard as pure sound like music. The meaning of words is lost. There are cases of people sustaining right hemisphere damage who retain the function of speech and the understanding of the speech of others, but have difficulty expressing emotions. Some can't distinguish sentences spoken with emotion. Still other patients lose the relationship between word meaning and word placement in sentences—the lexical or syntactical. Words do not have an intuitive relationship with their meaning. The implication is that the dysfunctional aspect has been 'disassociated' from the balance of the function. Sounds confusing, doesn't it? There is an almost unending, normal, temporary collaboration of very small and sometimes loosely organized areas of the brain.

My purpose here is not to document the entire fragmented organization of the brain beyond modularity. I will not attempt to provide an exhaustive list of all discrete, cohesive, modular assemblies of neurons. Instead, I will riffle through a few examples identified by research, grouping them by function. They seem counter-intuitive to any logically or cohesively operating nervous system. As noted above, these may be disassociated temporarily or, if permanently disassociated, lead to disabilities.

There are separate systems for the meaning of words and their sounds, the recognition of words in writing and print, the use of emotion in the sounds of speech, word placement in a sentence, and descriptions of objects and definitions of them.

Different aspects of language are managed in different systems: we can pronounce words without knowing how to spell them, read or write words without knowing how to pronounce them, and know what we want to say without necessarily being able to quite find the right word.

Sight and vision can fail in several ways while leaving the remaining aspects still operating. Signals of sight arriving at the occipital lobes are distributed to different areas for recognition of specific direction, forms, color, and general motion. There are separate systems for: color and gray—even in memory; moving and stationary subjects; meaning— pattern recognition in vision and vision itself; memory of inanimate and animate subjects.

Even perception reveals fragmentation. Damage to the visual cortex can cause patients to deny that they are blind. They do not 'perceive' they are blind and blame their poor vision on other factors like poor lighting. In other instances, damage to the brain has resulted in a person's inability to recognize their own disability—while not showing any other symptoms of delusional disorder.

Despite this fragmentation and independence of systems, we have an impression of cohesiveness. "I've got it together!" How does the brain give emergence to a mind that seems unified, that rises above this chaos? Network theory has identified a phenomenon called small worlds. Small worlds get the job done.

What are small worlds and what do they have to do with the brain? A small world can be thought of as a system that has random weak connections to other systems. Imagine a neighborhood gathering. It is a close community with strong ties as a consequence of various collaborating efforts in the neighborhood. One of the neighbors mentions she has a friend in China who has similar experience that could be useful on their next collaboration. She volunteers to e-mail her. The friend in China subsequently collaborates with the group in their efforts and then returns to obscurity. What does that have to do with the brain? The friend in China is a weak connection of the group—remotely located, but of use to the group! "My it's a small world!"

Random weak connections, augmenting the strong ones of a self-organizing group, enable clusters of elements to communicate directly without plodding through every link of every intervening system. These weak connections support the small worlds of life: Six Degrees of Separation, The World Wide Web, and the remotely separated systems of the brain. They occur randomly throughout natural and man-made systems. They substantially reduce the number of communication links, enabling rapid interaction between systems across distances. It is like an express connection—no local stops. Yet these weak connections have no effect on the organization of the communities they connect.

The Web illustrates still another aspect of CASs and network theory that is employed in the brain. If nodes are classified by the number of connections they have with other nodes, there is an inverse relationship between the number of nodes and the number of connections. Many nodes have few connections to others, but a very few nodes have many connections with other nodes. Mathematicians call this the power law.

These two characteristics of CASs show up in a multitude of systems including the brain.

This casual exploration of the brain's physical organization raises more questions than answers. How does it do its job in the blink of an eye? How does anything ever get done? What sequence of initial conditions and adjacent possibilities could have led to this state of affairs? What does all this mean for the future of the mind?

Evolution of the Brain

Since we are tracing the trajectory of pattern recognition in order to project that trajectory into the future, let's explore the evolution of the brain. The evolution of our brain, as of any CAS, has been a sequence of self-organizations, stimulated by environmental conditions. This evolution has occurred over millions of years. Several acquired capabilities mark fateful moves into adjacent possibilities. As much as science has researched these acquisitions, we don't know how they emerged: whether they developed separately or in some kind of collective symbiosis. In a sense, we are faced with an unresolvable chicken and egg question. Nevertheless we will discuss them separately here.

About 2.5 million years ago, our ancestors stood up. There was more to this than looking around and thinking, "Hey! This is cool!" It was not simply a vaudeville balancing act. Serious physical reorganization was required. The circulatory system reorganized to reliably and continuously pump blood uphill to the brain, and a good cooling system was required to vent the heat of the energy consumed.

Upright walking required a reorganization of the neural systems, too. Balance and orientation required reorganized motor systems and altered visual-motor collaboration. Our upright precursors likely tested variations of this new capability over millions of years.

Some believe that freeing the hands for other uses opened a sequence of adjacent possibilities leading to tool-making. Yet the evidence indicates a one million year stasis between the use of primitive tools and the development of sophisticated ones. The production of tools required the conception of the use and the end-product beforehand, and the coordination of efforts needed to make the tool. It required a reorganization of the collaboration of the neural systems, self-organizing through a whole new series of adjacent possibilities. Each step was probably an incremental advantage for survival in a changing environment.

Before exploring the implications of speech and language on neural reorganization, let us return to the brain's functional asymmetry. There is very little anatomical asymmetry in humans. True, my left arm is a quarter of an inch longer than my right, one foot is slightly larger than the other, and one ear is slightly higher than the other. But, this is nothing worth writing home about. In this respect, we are like other primates. In contrast, we have an enormous development of functional asymmetries in a physically symmetrical brain.

Just how important was this development? Our neocortex is 3.2 times the size of that of a chimp. The expansion occurred in the frontal and parietal lobes—both associated with our speech. If we consider the additional processing enabled by having different functions processed by different sides of the brain—the right temporal and the left temporal for example—it has been estimated that the cerebral potential has increased by 5.4 times without unduly increasing the size of the brain, birth hazards, dietary requirements, or heat dissipation needs.

The emergence of speech and language may have been the consequence of multiple factors. As we will see in Chapter 7, the sounds of speech and the concepts of language emerge from disparate, seemingly unconnected systems. Yet, each is required for the operation of the whole. The emergence of our ancestor was the culmination of a new level of complexity achieved in the brain's self-organization. Evidence of a phase transition is formidable.

Hidden among the more obvious reorganizations of the brain is one little discussed: memory. Memories are collaborations that engage the hippocampus in the limbic system. As we saw in Chapter 3, the systems of emotion participate in self-organizations throughout the brain. The hippocampus, home to fundamental residual patterns in the limbic system of the brain, is well connected with the neocortex, collaborating with virtually every self-organizing effort undertaken. The repeated 'firing' of a synapse in the hippocampus leads to an increase in the sensitivity of the neuron—this enhancement in sensitivity and signal transmission we identified in Chapter 4 as the Long Term Potentiation (LTP). The sensitivity also increases in synapses of collaborating neurons leading to memory strengthening. This characteristic was an early development in mammals, yet it plays a key role in our cognitive memory.

LTP is experience-specific. Zapping a specific set of connections between neurons affects only the synapses involved in that experience. LTP is a consequence of a sufficient number of synapse firings having occurred and of the level of stimulation that results from those firings. It is evidence of a well-trodden path. Multiple collaborations between multiple connections in a pattern establishes a common LTP between all participants, binding the entire collaboration together in a system. Any part of the system thereby becomes more sensitive to stimulation—even if a disturbance does not directly affect the balance of the residual pattern. This can result in subsequent stimuli from only one connection making a greater impression than before the joint stimulation—a means for associating experiences. It's as if the entire group has been put on alert so that a stimulation of one part of the group will alert all members. The very large number of interconnections from the hippocampus to the neocortex makes the hippocampus ideal for establishing associations between the different connections—between the different aspects of different experiences in time and space. These patterns—and the dominant characteristics of experience represented in them—respond to stimuli that may only partly be contained in the residual pattern. Only part of the residual pattern may be stimulated, but the LTP of the group will be affected through their LTP associations. We explored this same cross-stimulation phenomenon in Chapter 3. The stimulation of partial associations in memories are similarly candidates for metaphor—understanding one thing in terms of another.

Two other factors contribute to the tremendous increase in human cognitive memory. First, the human prefrontal cortex has an area that is more than five times that of apes. Secondly, much of human cognitive memory is encoded in language, increasing the capacity of memory. Encoding information at a conceptual level is extremely important to our story. We will explore this at length when we take up language.

Vision has its own chapter, yet we can note here that vision has wandered through its own sequence of adjacent possibilities with consequences both subtle and profound. While the visual cortex substantially increased in size from ape to man, we inherited an efficient system of sight complete with full binocular capability. It is in the extensive interconnectedness with the other areas of the brain that it is distinctive. The self-organizations of the systems giving emergence to vision have employed virtually the entire cerebral cortex in collaboration.

As the self-organizing of the visual system spread into adjacent possibilities, incorporating the collaboration of other self-organizing systems, other experiences, registrations and residuals, as the value of enhancing vision became so compelling, the visual experience came to dominate self. It is that experience that will dominate the future of mind.

Pulling It All Together

There was a long period of time before these capabilities began fully collaborating. We can only speculate how the testing of adjacent possibilities continued for millions of years before something approaching our present-day brain began to emerge.

After a long period of stasis, the subsequent rapid development in tool-making and the sudden flowering of the arts coincides with a period of rapid growth in the development of the prefrontal lobes of the brain— symptomatic of a phase shift. Science has associated the pre-frontal lobes with the thought process necessary for the perception of an application: visualizing the end product, imagining construction, identifying the raw materials, and holding these thoughts together during fulfillment. In the process, our ancestors changed from being passive reactors to the environment into active shapers of their environment, and this process eventually led to our own electronic augmentation of the environment.

While there are gaps in the fossil record, the size of the brain increased dramatically, too. The brain's size increased by a factor of three in only 2 million years. Our ratio of brain to body weight is 8 times that of primitive primates.

This is curious. Animals normally evolve no more than what they need to survive in their environment. A larger brain was a costly investment requiring increased energy supplies—the brain uses 20% of the body's energy—and new infrastructure to cool it.

What drove this incredible growth in the brain? We consider two candidates. It could have been one or the other... or both. The time of this enormous growth in the brain coincided with an era during which the climate varied markedly about every 10,000 years—and significant changes could take place in as little as a decade. A brain that could function in a variety of different, rapidly changing climates would be advantageous. The expansion of the neocortex, where routine planning and preparation are centered, would have provided the capacity for anticipating, planning for, and accommodating climate change that was occurring at a pace far too rapid for the body to adapt to. The time scale of physical evolution cannot accommodate the rapid climate changes of that period. But the repeated self-organizing of neural systems interacting with one weather extreme after another could lead to the emergence of whole new systems.

Second, moving into a hunting way of life with the need for planning, collaboration and improved motor-visual coordination, in response to the rapid climate change, would further stimulate the self-organizing of neural systems. It was a dynamic process, a cycle of events and self-organizing responses repeated over eons of time with each twist of the climate. It was a time of fantastic self-organizing exploration by CASs. The rapid environmental changes presented rapidly changing adjacent possibilities for exploration. The residual state of each self-organization rapidly incorporated new capabilities in response to the pressures of the environment. Because of these new capabilities, each residual state, the initial conditions for the next self-organization, presented a greater number of adjacent possibilities. This was a time for moving through the most adjacent possibilities and the most numerous means for getting into them—improving chances for survival. The rapid environmental changes of that era virtually whipped the neural systems into a frenzy of self-organization.

About 300,000 years ago, a crude model of *Homo sapiens* appeared. Our own model, dubbed by some *Homo sapiens sapiens*, emerged perhaps 70,000 years ago—certainly by 40,000 years ago. The brain of *Homo sapiens sapiens* was a CAS that combined the functions of observation, abstraction, and documentation. We see evidence of this in a trail tracked through art and artifacts.

Unlike primitive brains, as illustrated by the chimpanzee, our brain is distinguished by an overwhelming propensity for interconnection and collaboration. The brain's evolution through an increase in size seems to have given way to adjacent possibilities presented by interconnections. This may have been one more of nature's compromises: between a limiting birth canal and the advantage of more cognitive capacity. It is a brain of constant, persistent reorganization of neural elements seeking one another at all levels—and increasingly reaching out to collaborate with external systems.

Growing Up in the Neo-neocortex

The post-birth development of the brain has profound implications for the future. The growth in the size of the brain and the compromise between the size of the brain and the size of the birth canal have had evolutionary consequences that continue today. There is a delay in the brain's development until after birth. The process is effectively extended into the 'extra-placental' environment as the brain continues growth and development in the incubator of culture. The extreme immaturity of the human infant at birth requires more nurturing and time after birth than any other mammal. This immaturity also imposes costs on the group.

I will explore the evolution and implications of culture in more detail. But here we can note that systems of individuals, that is to say groups, also explored adjacent possibilities. Collaboration between individuals increased. Group living self-organized with consequences of value to the extra-placental development of the brain: cooperative parenting of infants; shared food and security; parenting of the young by the males; and more permanent pair-bonding. Other adjustments took place: the four phases of life for humans—infant, adolescent, reproductive, and post reproductive—are longer than for other primates.

The consequences of these changes are profound. The early years of an infant are exhilarating. The limitation on brain growth was effectively removed. Brain size increases from about 350cc at birth to about 1350cc in adults. After birth, the infant is literally making up its mind, making use of systems available at birth, expanding and augmenting those systems, interacting with the environment, exerting influence on the environment—all the time self-organizing through adjacent possibilities. Those little neurons are self-organizing like crazy! Key aspects of brain development are delayed until after birth: myelination—the insulation of the axons—dendritic development, and cellular maturation may not be completed until late childhood. New regions of the neocortex—the neo-neocortex—develop after birth in the context of the infant's environment. Six attributes of the neo-neocortex are worth noting here. It is a unique hominid development; it is the last module of the brain to evolve; it is the last module to mature; it has functional asymmetry; it maintains plasticity for learning in the development of the young; and it is associated with intellectual functions—including consciousness and self-consciousness, thinking, imagining, and creating.

The general speech areas in the human brain are formed before birth, but fine-tuning takes place after birth in the context of a cultural environment. As in all CASs, initial conditions and the sequence of self-organization make a difference. It becomes almost impossible to learn speech beyond the age of thirteen. The visual motor system is also waiting for further development after birth. The world after birth is a powerful influence on the physical development of the brain.

The human infant's life is learning-dependent. Language plays a key role in this learning. The child quickly learns to construct what we characterize as grammatically correct sentences, incessantly asking 'why?'. This acquisition of language in turn gives rise to levels of cognition far beyond anything imaginable in chimps.

Our brain continues self-organizing during a lifetime of exposure to cultural influence.

Suggested Additional Reading for Chapter 5

John Eccles, in *The Evolution of the Brain: Creation of the Self*, provides a thorough exploration of the physical brain. Joan Stiles, in *The Fundamentals of Brain Development*, discusses the sequence of brain development from pre-natal to post-adolescence, and the complementing programmed wax and wane of neural growth and destruction—a program that just happens to optimize the brain for furious environmental adaptation. William Calvin's *A Brain for All Seasons* is useful in understanding a process by which rapid and repeated climate change molded our brain.

Dean Falk in *Brain Dance*, and Elaine Morgan in *The Descent of the Child*, each provide a perspective on the trade-offs active in the great compromise between an ever larger brain and the limits of the birth canal.

Howard Gardner gives us a view of how culture shapes and prunes the brain's systems in *Frames of Mind: the Theory of Multiple Intelligences*. Lise Eliot provides observations on the developing brain in *How the Brain and Mind Develop in the First Five Years of Life*.

PART TWO

Vision and Emergence

We begin our exploration of emergent properties in part two with vision. That is appropriate since vision is the second principal force bearing on the future of the mind. We will continue part two with voice and language, more tangible emergent properties than vision. We will close part two by exploring the emergence of mind.

The exploration of the emergent properties of complex adaptive systems is a departure from the comfortably measured reality of the physical world.

The phenomenon of emergence is crucial to this story. Nevertheless, emergence is one of those unsatisfying phenomena in science. Cosmology has dark matter and dark energy—known only by their need to balance equations. Quantum Physics has virtual particles—also known by their need to balance equations, and entanglement—the spooky reality that two particles 'correlate' with one another instantaneously, seeming to violate the laws of classical physics. The Theory Of Everything has strings—none of which have been detected, and Complex Adaptive Systems have emergent properties—which have yet to be explained.

The origin of an emergent property is not predictable from an examination of the underlying self-organizing systems. Neither are its characteristics. Yet, emergence is within the context of a CAS. An emergent property is always *of* a CAS. Its origin is always a CAS.

Three emergent properties of specific CASs are of interest to us: vision, language, and mind. Exploring these will prepare us to consider The Future of The Mind.

We begin our journey into the metaphysics of emergence with the first virtual reality, vision.

CHAPTER 6

Vision

"See that!" "Where?", you say. No matter how you try, you can't pick it out. You feel foolish. Concentration? Focus? Or something else? Maybe you haven't *learned* to see 'it.' As we noted in Chapter 4, vision is learned. Remember those photons? What about them would tell you to see the softness in a brown fur, or the roughness of cement?

This is the first chapter in our exploration of the emergence of mind. Vision is more than sight. Sight registers what is stimulating the retina. The task of vision is to determine what is going on out there. Vision is an emergent property of those CASs comprising sight and their interactions with other CASs. Just as sight is a window on the brain, vision discloses aspects of emergence seen in the mind. It is not to be found in any one place, or solely within the body. Vision is a property that emerges without direction, without central control.

Following on from pattern-recognition, the faculty of vision is the second of three evolutionary trajectories influencing the future of the mind that we will explore. We are first and foremost visual creatures. Only vision can unite a complete, coherent concept of what is going on out there. Have you awakened to a noise in a dark room? You turn on the light to see what is happening out there. Perhaps you look out of the window, or go outside... to *see* what is happening. What's that grit in your food? Take it out of your mouth and look at it. You stumble and look back to see what is wrong with the sidewalk. Want to better understand a mathematical relationship? Graph it! In his book *Chaos*, Gleick shows us the consequences of nonlinearity, attractors and fractals with beautiful visualizations. We are visualizing creatures.

Seeing may seem simple, yet the process of vision is extremely complex. It has been widely studied by psychologists and neuroscientists, and mulled over by philosophers. It emerges from that interface for which the roles of sensation and perception are most difficult to distinguish. The interface supporting vision is now used principally for perception not sensing.

There are several facets of vision that are of interest. First, the systems giving rise to vision include sight, the broadband interface between me and the other side of the boundary. The physical interfaces of sight that are directly traceable to the faculty of vision, and those additional neural resources that interact with sight, far surpass those of any other interface with the environment. Secondly, vision is learned. It is a manifestation of repeated self-organizing in response to the environment, emerging in a sequential manner. Each environmental experience enriches the patterns of collaboration available for perception of what is going on out there. Initial conditions matter throughout development and use, but early experiences matter most. Thirdly, the objects of human vision are increasingly tailored to the strengths and idiosyncrasies of human vision... tailored by humans in ever tightening feedback. The world of nature is becoming just another 'window' as we spend hours each day in front of screens filled with objects we design specifically to attract our attention and entice our continued participation. These objects also have emergent properties that are manifest only in collaboration with human sight and vision. The display of my smartphone has an emergent meaning only if it is 'seen.' Fourthly, these objects are increasingly sustained electromagnetically. They are more virtual than real. Lastly, these virtual objects increasingly participate in our own self-organizations—in the laying down of residual patterns in the neural systems that give rise to vision.

There is ever more collaboration among electromagnetic systems and biological neural systems in ever tightening feedback. At what point does vision become an emergent property of both systems?

Where *is* Vision?

Reactions to what is happening at the retina have been traced to neural registrations throughout the brain. In the retina itself, neural systems begin parsing the initial interactions, categorizing dimensions of the stimulation for continuing analysis. An important aspect of vision is its ability to separate, to abstract objects of interest from the background. Vision of the outside world differs importantly from the projection of that world on the retina.

The eye, directed by vision, focuses on a narrow range with its sharpest focus; first on this, then on that; first looking close, then at a distance; scanning and exploring the environment. This active effort is the hallmark of visual perception. The retina both selects objects through the needle-like stare of the macula, and discriminates between them and the background falling outside that glare. Sight is informed by feedback from vision to further focus and discriminate. These interactions, shared with the neurological multitudes, are parsed into ever-increasing minutiae, enlist numerous fragments of residual patterns of other CASs, abstract distinct characteristics in the environment, and provoke collaboration between seemingly endless systems. The brain's vision-supporting areas become increasingly discriminating—and interconnected with other parts of the brain.

Vision is also informed by the other senses, by the emotions and the time-stamp of the body, and by the continuous self-reorganization of the complete neuronal network. Sounds, smells, touch—all contribute to the discriminating power of vision. The perception of form, surface properties, three-dimensional spatial relationships, and movement—the enrichment of what is going on out there—are emergent properties of collaborating, independent, physically separate systems, all working together in visual coherence.

For example, color is part of the overall visual perception. We do not see color in isolation. Experiments show that our perception of the color of an object can vary with the color of the background. Another dimension of vision is the ability to fill in the blanks—say the partial head and an ear glimpsed from behind across a crowded room at a party... vision completes the object... and there is the friend we seek. The photons have a lot of help.

It is clear that vision cannot exist without the environment: no environment, no photons, no transactions, no interactions, no emergence, and no vision. We must include in vision those systems of the environment with which sight interacts. This is not a requirement for sight. Irrespective of the presence or absence of environmental stimulation, the systems of sight are physically there—even if inert. Vision arises then from two interactive sets of systems: those internal to the nervous system, and those external ones in the environment. Vision draws together separate aspects of the object seen. Vision is a collaboration between different senses and the environment.

Even so, a careful examination of the systems directly linked to sight and those extensive portions of the brain that interact with sight do not reveal a central location where we 'see.' Furthermore, research shows that vision can be altered in many ways without complete failure—and with *no* alteration of the systems of sight. Conversely, when sight is artificially inverted, vision will adjust to present a normal aspect. The additional readings include numerous clinical examples in which some aspect of vision fails in the presence of fully functioning sight. The self-organizations and the residuals that sight leaves behind are only physical manifestations of the interactions at the retina—changes in the physical properties of biological components. The cognitive faculty we characterize as vision has no central location within us. The location of vision itself is elusive, if it exists at all.

Vision is the first, seemingly real, virtual reality.

How Does Vision Develop?

The book *Crashing Through: A True Story of Risk, Adventure, and the Man Who Dared to See*, relates the experience of a 46-year-old man who recovered his sight after 43 years of blindness—and then struggled to regain his vision. His systems of sight were restored; photons were being registered, images were complete and clear, but the collaboration of other neural systems necessary for the emergence of vision was stunted. How could this be?

Vision is unique among the properties emerging from the five senses. Vision begins development only after birth. At first light, at birth, the chaos of the environment's light bombards the retina. Neural systems self-organize in response to a mélange of primitive artifacts—edges, angles, colors, and motion. Residual patterns of shapes and forms come together. Vision defines and differentiates objects with experience and recurrence. Initial conditions—patterns—are established, adjacent possibilities are explored in self-organizations, patterns overlap and coalesce, shapes are registered. Resonating self-organized patterns arise and a bias—LTP—in their favor emerges. What has been registered repeatedly, resonantly, will be registered more easily, with more intensity, and without the need for so much stimulation. The residual patterns of objects overlap and self-organize with other neural systems in expanding collaborations that form groups, sub-groups, and super-groups. Relationships between them become deep-seated and pervasive. Initial conditions are organized for a lifetime.

The role of vision is to assess what is changing out there. Vision requires interpretation of more than the physical interaction with photons at the retina boundary, more than the resonance of residual patterns in the systems of sight. Vision requires a history—a set of residual patterns of what has happened to me coincident with what has happened out there. Vision depends on experience with the environment. Vision is most subject to, and most influenced by, the environment in which it develops post-birth.

Research indicates that the development of vision in infants begins at birth and follows a sequential progress. It involves more than learning to focus the eyes. Newborns will turn their heads toward a sound indicating that they expect to see something. Infants are able to relate the particular feel of an object to its visual image. They can determine which visual display matches what they hear and they look longer at a display that moves in sync with the sound. In the first few months, babies use edges and patterns of movement to separate objects, know how the objects moved, know that the objects are part of a three-dimensional space, and can link information from different senses. By the age of nine months, babies are able to solve simple puzzles such as finding a ball hidden behind your back.

If the development of vision fails to begin, or is in some way arrested, if the sequence is interrupted, vision will not develop properly, if at all— even though the systems of sight are unimpaired. Vision must experience the initial conditions that will forever enable and delimit what we see.

The adjacent possibilities of future vision come into being during infancy.

Ways of Seeing

Sight can be excruciatingly exact—both discriminating and comprehensive. It self-organizes the residuals of actual environmental stimulation. Sight is the medium of record. Yet, vision is a mashup—emerging from an agglomeration of disparate systems and interests pulling together and apart for an occasion. Vision assays and extrapolates the present based on the experiences of a multitude of self-interested systems with residuals. It assigns significance to what is happening out there. Vision can be seduced, misled. Vision can be wrong.

What we see with our vision depends on what is happening on the other side of the boundary that is 'me.' What we see also depends on what we have learned to see—what provoked our internal systems to link up and interact during their initial self-organizing search for one another. What we see depends on the resonance of residual patterns linked to what we expect to see. Residual patterns and collaborating systems fill in and augment the interaction of sight with experience. Differences in initial conditions, in experiences, make a difference to how we see and what we see. What we see as infants—what our environment offers—determines *how* we see forever after. Vision is learned from the interaction of neural systems inside the body, and the external systems available for interacting. The adjacent possibilities of initial sequences of self-organizations—of the initial residual patterns of experience—slowly but inexorably limit what we will see. Kittens, as we noted in the chapter on sight, deprived of experiences with horizontal lines during their development are unable to see stairs when mature.

What we see depends on the context from which we look. The external stimulating systems include not only physical surroundings, but community and culture; the artifacts, and habits of the community; and the contexts of seeing that are indigenous to the culture. Cultural and physical influences in early development—either applied or deprived—establish the bounds of lifelong vision. The elements and capabilities of vision vary between cultures and communities. The community includes those systems internal to each of its other members—the systems of relatives, friends and interacting strangers. What we see is influenced by what we are taught to see, what we expect to see, what we anticipate, what we are looking to see.

I experienced this on the Serengeti as our guide Wyrobi pointed to the distant horizon and said "simba." Across the Serengeti, through the 20 x zoom of my digital camcorder, was a speck on the horizon. The speck grew larger and as legs were hinted in the view finder he said "male." As a slightly rounded head emerged on the top of the stick figure in the viewfinder he said "eight years old." In time a magnificent male lion with a gorgeous ruff approached to within yards of our Landrover. Giving us a look that clearly said "gawd, more tourists," this magnificent lion turned, bounded up into a kopje of rock, turned his back on us, and went to sleep. How could Wyrobi, a Maasai born on the grasslands of the Serengeti see what I couldn't? What was the secret?

Maasai can distinguish lions at hundreds of yards. Inuits can identify many different kinds of snow. Some cultures see only two colors—green and everything else. Culture places nature in just another 'window.' How did *you* learn to see...

Our emotional condition also influences vision—our body's state of being, our body's preparedness to see. The context of the body from which we look influences our vision. The hallucinations of vision are body-based.

Abstraction and Metaphor

Earlier I said that vision abstracts. What does that mean? Essentially, features or characteristics are taken out of—or more accurately used—without, context. So why is that important? This abstracting aspect of vision is also essential to metaphor.

In Chapter 3 we read that "metaphor is understanding and experiencing one kind of thing in terms of another." A metaphor, by abstracting certain features of an experience, diminishes the importance of other features of the experience... like the context in which it happens.

Both vision and metaphor discriminate: they abstract. They selectively highlight some things and they diminish the importance of the rest. In its simplest form, we might say that vision removes or abstracts objects or features from their background for emphasis, focus, or for specific attention in the moment.

An example perhaps would be recognizing the partial pattern of a predator moving in high grass based on the experience of seeing the complete pattern of one move in the open. These residual patterns and their collaborators—in whole or in part—are subject to enlistment by other overlapping, or higher-level patterns. They are available for use in systems that self-organize in other contexts. They are a limitless source for metaphor. And those patterns are increasingly stimulated by our augmenting, cyberous devices.

The Emergence of Vision

When faced with the what, where, when, why and how of vision, we don't really know much. We know a great deal about sight. Research indicates the relationship of vision to sight, but it also indicates a more complicated relationship with vast areas of the brain beyond sight. We have concluded that we do not know where vision is. So I close this chapter by acknowledging that we do not know the how of vision either. We can characterize vision as an emergent property of a CAS. We can say that vision emerges from experience—from the CASs formed by the connection and interaction of systems internal to the brain as well as those systems pervasive throughout the external environment. But we don't know how.

Visual perception lays the groundwork for concept formation. Visual perception is concerned with grasping generalities and specifics, with kinds of qualities, objects, and events. Vision is of the stimulation of the eyes, and operates with a vast range of residual patterns from a multitude of collaborating, perhaps weakly connected, neural systems. Vision organizes all of this in the context of the experience of life—the resonance of current perception and stored experience, in the residual patterns of prior self-organizations. Somehow, it emerges.

For an engineer, that is as satisfying as the virtual particles of quantum physics, and the dark energy of cosmology. We must wait for science to advance its understanding of CASs.

Suggested Additional Reading for Chapter 6

See *The Embodied Mind*, by Francisco Varela, Evan Thompson, and Eleanor Rosch, for an exploration of the sources and attributes of visual perception. They, as well as Richard Restak in *The Modular Brain*, explore vision as the interactions of sight with other systems and the seeming incongruity of the failure of vision without the failure of the other systems and the converse. Bruno Breitmeyer, in *Blindspots: The Many Ways We Cannot See*, discusses the importance of sight's interaction with the environment—the initial conditions and adjacent possibilities, and the importance of sequence in the development of vision.

In *Visual Thinking*, Rudolf Arnheim uses art as a perspective for exploring the collaborative effort of visual perception, where the brain, enlisting the efforts of other neural systems and the environment in which they operate, fills in the blanks left by sight. He also provides an analysis of abstraction as a sensory activity.

For a hands-on report of visual learning in infants, see *The Scientist in The Crib: What Early Learning Tells us About the Mind,* by Allison Gopnick, Andrew Meltzoff, and Patricia Kuhl.

Robert Horn shows us how inseparable and influential evolving visual techniques of communication have become to vision and understanding, in *Visual Language: Global Communications for the 21st Century.*

For the experience of a 46-year-old man who recovered his sight after 43 years of blindness—and then struggled to regain his vision, see *Crashing Through: A*

True Story of Risk, Adventure, and the Man Who Dared to See, by Robert Kurson.

Emergence: Contemporary Readings in Philosophy and Science, edited by Mark Bedau and Paul Humphreys, provides a discussion of emergence from several philosophical and scientific sources.

CHAPTER 7
Voice and Language

The elevator door opened and she stepped into the corridor. "Hey, did you see that article in the Journal this morning?" Without breaking stride he grinned and replied, "It said it all, didn't it?" Two sentences, seventeen words, and to the right people, an enormous transfer of information—loaded with concepts and shared experience. It happens every day, all day, neatly wrapped patterns of sounds transporting whole litanies of patterns—concepts and experience—across empty space from one person to another, from one mind to another, or from one to many. Our world is filled with sounds.

Humans are very good at using sounds and machines are not. During lunch one day at MIT's Media Lab, Marvin Minsky gave an example of an everyday conversation that he said would have been impenetrable to artificial intelligence. "Where is my pen?" he asked. His wife responded, "It's in the bathroom behind where the Q-tips used to be."

So why are sounds a part of this story? Why are voice and language of interest as we trace the trajectory of vision into the future of mind? There are two reasons. Sounds give us another opportunity to explore the hierarchical aspects of CASs, but the principal reason is that sounds are integral to the patterns representing concepts, the raw material of cognition. In this respect, language is a rival of vision as we become more visually oriented—as the patterns of our cognition become ever more linked to visual interfaces for exchange with other CASs. Before language, before the sounds of mind, vision was the tool of cognition. Originating in self-organizing patterns, sounds are a means for compressing whole concepts. Sounds, and the language they make up, are the zip files of experience. The sounds of mind are intricately interwoven into the very essence of the concepts in mind. When we think, it is with the sounds of mind, with language. The patterns of sounds, as used in language, are a projection of our neuronal registrations and collaborations—of our very own residual patterns—into the environment. Language is an interface for sharing experience between like-minded CASs. Language is a phase transition that opened into a whole sequence of adjacent possibilities. Now vision, augmented by CASs that are 'not me,' is reasserting its role in cognition. How will the sounds of mind play out in the future of a mind increasingly governed by vision? Will the sounds of mind in the patterns of cognition constrain the future of vision-dependent mind? How are the adjacent possibilities limited?

Let's begin with an exploration of our investment in the use of sounds and language, for it is a heavy investment, indeed.

The Basic Physical Components

The voice is a Rube Goldberg agglomeration of other-focused, unrelated systems that just happen to be there when we want to express language. The voice demonstrates the derivative use by CASs of independent systems having other functions. The inherent risks they bring underscore the importance of language. The life-supporting role of the respiratory system is to get oxygen into our bodies and poisonous gases out. It is incidentally the source of acoustic energy for the voice.

It is also a convenient process for injecting ourselves *into* the environment. The configuration of our oral cavity—the larynx, tongue, palate and jaw—intended for chewing and swallowing, extrinsically gives us the ability to produce unique sounds. The risk is that everything we eat passes over a poorly protected, dangerously placed, breathing tube: an opportunity for dangerous confusion. We are more likely to choke while eating than any other animal.

In Control

Speech requires the controlled expulsion of air for acoustic energy. We are not unique in our ability to make sounds. We are uncommon in why we make them. The calls or warnings of other primates are the responses integral to emotions. The sounds are in that sense involuntary. Without emotion, vocalization is extremely difficult for other primates. The sounds of speech are deliberate. This is the 'ante-up' of our speech production.

We inherited from non-human primates complex neural systems that are able to reconfigure physical components in the interests of survival.

They manage muscle control for smooth sequencing of learned, skilled movements such as chewing and swallowing, and they produce oral-facial expressions, even skilled hand movements. In humans, they have also self-organized to manipulate the same muscles for the composition of sounds, to coordinate the smooth, learned muscle sequences of the voice.

At an early age, infants begin playing with their hands and feet and, in the process, self-organizing neural patterns collaborate, learning muscle control. Infants also begin playing with sounds—cooing and ooing, learning the interaction and collaboration of their vocal tract with the voluntary control of breathing. That simple capability sets humans apart. We can exhale at the precise moment, the exact amount of air required to energize the elements of the vocal tract to produce precisely the sounds we want. On demand!

The neural systems involved in the production of speech underscore still another aspect of CASs. Collaborating systems enter into different kinds of behavior at different times: skilled hand movement, arm or leg movement, facial expression, and the motor actions for producing speech. These neural systems also collaborate in hearing sounds, in receiving speech. The neural systems of the brain are anxious to collaborate in activities with an adeptness that can explore adjacent possibilities in concert with other systems in real time.

There is a bonus in the exploration of voice and language: it gives us an opportunity to elaborate on the oft repeated "CASs self-organize in hierarchies." How? Each of the physical systems involved in producing voice is manipulated by a separate and distinct system of the brain. Each is managed by a separate and distinct self-organizing, pattern-registering system with a mission other than that of producing the voice. These independent neural systems, acting as basic elements themselves, have self-organized into a higher order system—jointly managing a mélange of disparate, other-directed physical systems in order to produce the sounds of voice. This 'super-system,' in turn self-organizing with that set of systems from which concepts emerge, produces the conceptual expression of sound that we call language.

Several layers of CASs in the brain—collaborating to bring us sounds and language—are revealed. There are those neuronal systems independently self-organizing in support of separate physical tasks such as breathing, chewing, swallowing, or smiling. Then these same elemental neuronal systems join in self-organization to manipulate those same physical systems to produce sounds: voice. In another stack of neurons, elemental systems self-organize to register basic experiences. These elemental systems in turn self-organize into patterns of concepts. Then the whole shebang—the voice systems and the concept systems—self-organizes to bring us the emergence of language. While this is a gross oversimplification of the extraordinary dance of the CASs involved, it illustrates the uncanny ability of CASs to participate as the basic elements in the self-organization of still other systems, building hierarchies of systems along the way.

Now back to sounds and language.

Evolution—Timing and Sequence

Why were voice and the emergence of language so important that we risked our lives for them? We do not know. Nevertheless, the fossil record, the artifacts of our ancestors, and observations made of other primates, are all suggestive. As our ancestors grew in number, self-organizing into large groups for security and survival—they overscheduled! Three factors have been advanced for inclining self-organization toward the adjacent possibilities of voice and language.

1. Other primates depend on grooming for maintaining the relationships of group dynamics. That's how they keep in touch. As groups increased in size, there was insufficient time to maintain relationships through grooming. Language would have provided an alternative.

2. Tool-making added another dimension to survival. Yet, for over a million years, there was little improvement in tools. Each tool was a new invention. Language would have provided a means for sharing knowledge, improving tools, and bettering the group's chances of survival.

3. Finally, sharing experience and knowledge would have been advantageous for hunting and gathering, too. Language would provide a means for exchanging information, planning, and identifying members of a community.

A series of small changes, movements through adjacent possibilities, advantageous even at the margins, led to the human supralaryngeal. The sequence of change was critical. Newborn infants experience the sequence today. They begin life with an ape-like supralaryngeal—optimizing eating and minimizing potential choking. They can make only a limited range of sounds. By the age of three months, most infants have improved control of eating and swallowing as the supralaryngeal grows, repositioning the larynx down the throat for improved vocalization. This physical reconfiguration continues through adolescence, including one of those embarrassments of puberty, the breaking or squeaky voice.

Evidence suggests there were multiple self-organizations through a long sequence of adjacent possibilities taking place haltingly, independently and in parallel, over 2–3 million years, culminating between forty and a hundred thousand years ago.

The Performance Package

There is more. Not only are the sounds of mind and language important to the compression of concepts in cognition, they must be extremely important for communication between us. We have developed a high performance package, a system that is fine-tuned for understanding one another under a vast array of circumstances and at a pace that is remarkable. Yet, we are totally unaware of these distinctive, important attributes in our production of voice.

We do not really hear what is said. Well, we do, but we don't. The transactions of the sound waves from the speaker at the ear are accurate, but the perception, the registration, is *derived* from what is heard. The shape of the human vocal tract is not the most elegant instrument for producing sound. It does not produce a single frequency. Various frequencies form acoustic patterns that are the primary determinants of the sounds of speech. Nevertheless, for any given configuration of the system there is a sweet spot generating one frequency among the others that contains the majority of the energy. Those studying the acoustic characteristics of the voice call these formant frequencies. It is this formant frequency having the most energy that we 'hear.' Then in collaboration with the residual patterns of our experience, the full acoustic patterns of the speaker are derived from these formant frequencies. The energy we perceive is a collaboration of the transactions and experience with the sounds of various speakers, in various emotional or bodily states, and under various circumstances.

This has the effect of increasing understanding under a wide range of circumstances and sources.

The systems registering acoustic energy resonate throughout their residual patterns of experience. As a consequence of this performance package, humans perceive these patterns of sound at rates four to twenty times faster than they perceive any other sounds and faster than the perception of sounds by any other animal! That can be important in responses for survival, or at a noisy party.

Furthermore, our sounds are unique, non-nasal sounds. These are less subject to misinterpretation than nasal sounds. They form sharp peaks of acoustic energy with more stability resulting in fewer errors and greater fidelity during times of system stress—nature's error correction/detection coding. The systems accommodate the hoarseness of a sore throat, the stopped-up sound of a head cold, the high-pitched sound of excitement and the intimacy of a whisper. Furthermore, our collaborative sound-making system fails gracefully—impaired systems can produce recognizable sounds and some systems continue functioning as others deteriorate.

The Sounds of Mind

But what of the importance of sounds of mind—of language—to vision and to the future of the mind? We make sounds to project ideas into the environment. We thrust our own patterns of concepts outward, to others. In a culture—in a group of humans relating as CASs—common sounds represent shared experiences of ideas or actions. These sounds register neural patterns that become an integral, collaborative part of the patterns of the concepts themselves. In the self-organizing system of neuronal patterns those of sound are as much a part of a concept as the pattern registered by the concept itself. The patterns of concept and sound self-organize into units such as: 'Sunset,' 'Career,' 'Half-baked,' 'Supernova,' and 'Love.' These sounds compress tens, hundreds, even thousands of words or sounds into one brief puff of air. These patterns are used integrally with, and as, the concepts they compress. Imagine the difference in suggesting that you share a sunset with that special person compared to sharing the orange ball in the blue sky with horizontal clouds of purple, gray, orange and red passing in front of the ball that is slowly dropped below the horizon—or some other such description.

The integrating patterns of sound demonstrate still another tendency of

CASs to self-organize in hierarchies. The residual patterns that represent my experience of what is going on out there collaborate with the residual pattern of the sounds of language associated with the experience. This results in a self-organization that subsumes all of the registrations. There is a tendency with language to self-organize other patterns with those of sounds, identifying, naming, characterizing, categorizing—in order to share with other members of the community. The patterns of sound insinuate themselves into every experience registered—activated by virtually every transaction with the environment. Tree, Body, Sour, Sweet, Stink, Caress, Sunset, Symphony, Tired, Yesterday, Rose. Names are the sound-enmeshed registrations of ideas, of interactions and transactions at all boundaries. These sounds encapsulate hierarchies of patterns. These sounds represent the vast set of patterns of which they are only a part. They are zip-filed relationships of experience. These sweeping sound-based concepts resonate through countless systems and hierarchies, simultaneously evoking patterns both minute and vast in scope. It is these encapsulating patterns of sounds that we call language.

These sounds transfer concepts between CASs with ease—internally within our own neuronal systems and, externally, within our community. The very concepts of our thoughts are compressed into the sounds of words, of language. When is the last time you 'thought' without the use of words, the sounds of mind? Our thoughts are a constant mélange of sounds transferring—competing, coalescing, and building. They are readily accessible, effortlessly projected, easily exchanged, and quickly identifiable experiences of the environment that are common to the CASs that share an environment. Sound has become a facile access, a ready resonator for hierarchies of neural patterns.

The mind relies on sound. These neural patterns of sound are collaborative, in the modes of initial interactions and transactions, body stamped, resonating, rife with feedback, and hierarchical. These patterns participate in the day-in, day-out self-organizing of neural patterns, in the registrations of experience, in the collaboration of hierarchical systems, and in the emergence of mind. They are the sounds of mind. How will these sounds of mind cohabit with the increasing influence of the patterns of vision?

Language is Learned

The sounds of language, the sounds of mind mold the self-organizing of post-birth development. What we hear and learn to say introduces us to concepts that will be with us for a lifetime. Language is the product of bootstrap self-organizing in concert with like-minded, already self-organized CASs—adults. Two dimensions are of interest to the future of the mind: the self-organizing of the systems enabling language, and the environment interacting with those systems.

Eons of movement through adjacent possibilities have led to neuronal systems having a facile capacity for interacting with distinctive sounds. They are pre-disposed to self-organize in response to the unique sounds of language, self-discovering the conduct of collaboration.

The initial residual patterns of acoustic experience limit the adjacent possibilities of the future. If infants do not hear language spoken in their first years, they will never learn to speak it properly. The concepts compressed into the sound of words can be lost forever. Yet, a child can easily learn two or three languages. It is more difficult for adults to learn a new language.

The sequential development and hierarchical nature of language is evident in the emergence of language in infants. As sounds open adjacent possibilities, and eliminate others, unused connections wither, reducing the ability to register the sounds of other languages.

The learning of language is coincident in time with learning vision. Infants begin learning language long before they begin to talk. The first challenge to infants lies in the registrations of neural patterns in the brain. The sounds of language are not discrete and separable. Mouths of different sizes and shapes make different sounds intending the same meaning. We may speak quickly, or slowly, be hoarse or excited. People speaking different languages hear very different sounds.

One-month-old babies distinguish sound contrasts and categories of sounds for every language and speaker. At about three months babies coo—they know something about participating in dialogue. At the age of seven or eight months, they begin a babbling that is identical in all languages. They self-organize mouth-to-sound relationships, relating voice-generating components with the sounds produced. Between 6 and 12 months, infants self-organize categories of sounds in the interactions with adults around them. They self-organize with the language of the environment. Prototypes enable the registration of indistinct sounds, but disadvantage other-language sounds.

At the age of nine months, babies show a preference for the sound combinations common in their environment. They learn the singsong patterns of words before they learn the words themselves. It is only after they register the sounds common in their environment that they learn which combinations are common. Registering common combinations makes it possible to divide the continuous stream of sound into words, even if they do not know what those words mean. By 12 months, the registered sounds begin self-organizing into perceived words that seemed hidden in the constant stream-without-pause of sounds in the environment.

The hierarchical self-organization accelerates as the neuronal patterns—the experience-base—grows. At 18 months, they actively restructure the language to suit their needs. They will use a word and a structure they have registered and shape it to a new experience. They begin to use language as their own. Before the age of three, children put words together to make new sentences and create meanings that are more complex. At this phase, they have already self-organized some grammar: different orders of the same words can have different meanings. At the age of 4 or 5, children are well on their way to mastering the language of their environment.

Language self-organizes in a culture. Infants have an incredible language-learning support system in adults. When speaking to infants, adults in every culture use a voice that is animated, warm, high pitched, very melodic, sing-song, slow and exaggerated, and with lengthened vowels. Motherese. All of us do it. Motherese sentences are shorter, simpler, and repetitious with slight variations. In all cultures, Motherese is more clearly pronounced than adult conversation.

Old Habits are Difficult to Break

Adjacent possibilities are bound to the unique sounds of language. The sounds of speech have been given a visual presence in writing. Nevertheless, writing represents sounds. Writing is tremendously empowering—but writing is not about letters, not about words. Writing is about the use of letters and words as expressions of sounds. Writing represents coded speech, encoded sounds. Written words are a cue to sounded words, real or imagined, directly or indirectly. We use these cues by reading—either aloud or 'in our heads'. We will return to this in Chapter 9, Sensuous Interfaces.

Reading may be syllable by syllable. It may be accelerated using speed-reading techniques. Written words may be augmented with color, flashing lights, illustrations, even music. They may be chiseled in stone or presented electronically. Even so, written words are ultimately related to sound in order to find meaning. The sounds of mind are rooted in speech, in sound.

At about the age of 18 months, babies go into an intense period of naming things, categorizing things with sounds—zip-filing whole concepts. The insinuation of sounds throughout the labyrinth of the brain's neuronal patterns assumes a new hierarchical intensity. Objects, actions—whole registered experiences—are bound together with the sounds of language. Concepts integrated in the sounds of language, and the artifacts of culture in post-birth development, are sound-dependent.

Children deprived of learning language do not have access to the symbolic and emotional life of a community. The mental and physical processes underlying social behavior do not self-organize. Patterns of sounds are inextricably linked with the bundles of other registered patterns, the experiences and social interactions that comprise the everyday interaction of language users. Language integrates individuals into a larger CAS with meaning and purpose. Language binds us together. Language binds our concepts. The mind labors within the bounds of the sounds of language. Even—and especially—the objects of vision are wrapped in the sound of names. We have all experienced the toddler's delight in naming everything she sees. The use of language would be very difficult to replace.

Sounds and Words in the Visual Mode

Culture has given a visual dimension to language, to the sounds of mind. The visual representation of sounds in writing and print has both elaborated and encroached on the influence of sound. Sound is manifest in the blaring, blinking, colorful, intrusive world of our self-created visual media. Even so, this visual expression represents sounds, sounds that in turn capture zip-filed concepts. The visualization of sound is still subject to translation into the sounds of mind.

Will the sounds of mind constrain visual cognition—and the future of the mind?

Suggested Additional Reading for Chapter 7

Philip Lieberman's *Uniquely Human* explores the unique systems underlying the human voice, particularly the performance package, the secondary use of disparate elemental systems, and the importance of the sequence of initial conditions.

Guy Deutscher, in *The Unfolding of Language: An Evolutionary Tour of Mankind's Greatest Invention,* presents the evolution of language moving along the edge of chaos, balanced between chaos and order, and explores the hierarchical nature of language.

Terrence Deacon explores the evolution of language and symbols through the hierarchical self-organization of language and the mind in *The Symbolic Species: The co-evolution of language and the brain.*

Tim Megarry, in *Society in Prehistory: the Origins of Human Culture*, explores the many attributes inherited by *Homo sapiens* from pre-historical ancestors, including the vocal system and the importance of an infant's social integration to learning language.

The Scientist in the Crib, by Allison Gopnick, Andrew Meltzoff, and Patricia Kuhl, and Lise Eliot's *How the Brain and Mind Develop in the First Five Years of Life*, provide perspectives on the learning of language by infants.

CHAPTER 8

The Emergence of Mind and Self
A Legacy of Complex Adaptive Systems

Having prepared ourselves with explorations of the emergence of vision, and of speech and language, we turn now to the emergence of mind.

Despite centuries of systematic study by scientists and philosophers, neither a generally accepted definition nor description of mind exists. Most investigators have focused on the model we humans currently have. This is not particularly helpful when exploring changes in the mind over time. Nevertheless there is a substantial amount of inter-disciplinary information demonstrating changes over time and a few of those who have explored the mind itself have chosen to focus on this aspect. Some of this work is noted in the suggested additional reading.

How did this phenomenon of mind begin? Some investigators have traced the mind as it eased through numerous adjacent possibilities over eons of time. They reveal the opportunistic nature of CASs, and phase shifts to whole new qualitative capabilities. We will explore investigations of three aspects of that change: increasing intelligence; changing processes of mind's internal representation; and mind's increasing versatility. We will also consider an increasingly intense self-referential focus—me. Each provides a different perspective on changes that have occurred in mind over time. Each suggests a dimension of the future of the mind.

We will interpret this work in the context of mind as an emergent property of CASs—emerging from self-organizing systems within the central nervous system in conjunction with systems of the environment.

Increasing Intelligence

Here, I am using the term 'intelligence' to describe the capacity of mind to change behavior following experience of environmental disturbances. I characterize these as decisions of the type *if-then... or—if* this, *then* that... *or* that, *or* maybe even that depending on a history of experience with the environment! The systems giving rise to the emergence of mind grew from simple *if-then* neural responses into incomprehensibly vast, intricate, networked hierarchies with numerous alternative reactions to *if*, depending on the history of experience with the environment. *Or* became significant in the emergence of mind. Perhaps a current example might be: *if* I see a ball coming toward me, *then* catch it... *or* return it across the net... *or* kick it back down the field... *or* stop my car because a child may be following it into the street. My experience with the environment is key.

If-then systems initially self-organized in the context of modality-specific disturbances and responses. The rules were simple: *if* this disturbance occurs, *then* this response. If touched, then recoil! Responses did not change with experience, with repeated disturbances.

It is as if increasing intelligence cycled through a period of special intelligence into a more general intelligence and then back into another kind of special intelligence. Three phases of mind changing through adjacent possibilities have been identified, each culminating in notable phase shifts increasing the capacity of mind for changing behavior with experience—phase shifts of increasing intelligence. These reorganizations have been marked in the behavior of other, surviving species, and in the artifacts of hominids.

What were the initial conditions preceding subsequent increases in intelligence? Initially systems were likely to have been responsive to specific conditions or circumstances—predisposed self-organizing systems that got the job done in the past: a frog flicking her tongue to capture an errant insect. It is likely these systems were modified very little, if at all, by experience. If this disturbance is registered, then this response is made. No matter how many insects fly near, the response is to flick her tongue. Responses were limited to separate systems operating in isolation from one another. Systems self-organizing for the acquisition of food would have had no connection with those self-organizing in order to seek shelter and security, or promote reproduction.

Increasing Intelligence—Phase 1

Then about 50–60 million years ago, a phase shift changed the world forever. In this first phase, these separate, isolated systems began to collaborate with one another, self-organizing into shared residuals, linked experiences. Modifications were likely to have been simple, with frequent errors. Perhaps food in areas inhabited by predators might be foregone in favor of more secure sources. Nevertheless, this capacity for using residual patterns of *multiple* experiences to modify behavior in current situations was an enormous change. The residual patterns of self-organizing systems, say of food acquisition, security and shelter, began self-organizing collaboratively, providing more extensive resonance with the environment, more encompassing registration of what is happening out there, enabling a major shift in qualitative response to that environment. This qualitative change in behavior was a phase shift in the self-organization of neuronal systems.

Systems emerging from this phase shift were still driven principally by separate systems, yet integrated into an overall set of patterns. Resonance and feedback slipped through overlapping patterns, perhaps woven together with the gossamer web of weak connections. Pattern recognition was no longer constrained to specific systems. The experience of disturbances to multiple systems together modified behavior in an integrated, more general-purpose—yet still limited—system giving rise to the mind. The lemur today preserves this phase of intelligence. The modality specific, or specialist type of intelligence began to give way to a measure of collaborative, general purpose intelligence.

Increasing Intelligence—Phase 2

The second phase shift was characterized by a return to specialization, but of a different nature. Functionally specific systems self-organized, augmenting the limited general intelligence attained in Phase 1. They self-organized in response to clusters of disturbances such as: group collaboration; the location, identification and storage of food; and the manipulation of environmental objects—tool-making. Working together was a qualitative shift in the response to environmental disturbances. Yet, the experience acquired by these systems responding to clusters of environmental disturbances, of experience in one functional area, had little influence on the *responses* in another. The lessons learned from group cooperation for providing security did not influence behavior in the acquisition of food. At a primitive level, this phase is reflected today in monkeys and chimpanzees.

There were several tryouts in adjacent possibilities before the third phase shift occurred. Of the various experiments in the fossil record, three have received particular attention. *Homo habilis* appeared about two million years ago, leaving no evidence of a capacity for integrating functional behaviors. *Homo erectus* presided over a million-year-long stasis in tool-making—not a strong recommendation for breakthrough. Not even archaic *Homo sapiens* pulled it all together.

Increasing Intelligence—Phase 3

It was only about 100,000 years ago that evidence of a sweeping phase shift unifying all aspects of acquired experience began to fill the record. All aspects of the mind began clicking together in *Homo sapiens*. Acquired experience and knowledge were applied across all aspects of interaction with the environment. This phase shift brought much more than registration and recognition of patterns stimulated by the environment. The extensive interconnectivity, overlap and agglomeration of experiential patterns and augmenting external storage enabled the self-organizing of extra-environmental experiences—patterns of experience *that had not been, perhaps could not have been, experienced*. These systems self-organized so as to provide patterns internally provoked by the self-organizing of the systems themselves. Disturbances were registered, but not from the boundary of 'me,' but rather from the boundaries of systems within 'me.' Residual patterns self-organized, but not in response to external environmental disturbances, rather in response to stimulation from systems self-organizing within 'me.' This was a truly profound qualitative change in intelligence. *Our* model of mind had arrived—the mind of art, symbols, and imagination.

The Changing Processes of Neuronal Representation

The processes by which environmental disturbances are represented in our neuronal patterns have changed in character over time, too. As neuronal CASs self-organized through adjacent possibilities, the emerging mind capitalized on the opportunities it was presented with. Changes in pattern-representing processes provide another perspective on the evolution of mind.

Pattern registration—the character of the neuronal representation of environmental disturbances—is key. Change in the process or character of neuronal representation is implied by innovations in culture—as manifested in behavior and artifacts. We use 'culture' to describe the rules and properties supporting self-organizing communities of minds—minds which are, themselves, CASs. Culture and neuronal representation, if not symbiotic, are circular in their relationship. Importantly, past innovations in culture can indicate what we might expect of the mind in the future. An examination of the behaviors and artifacts of cultures through time has suggested three phase shifts in the process of neuronal representation as manifested in these changes in culture.

Apes provide a baseline. Apes live entirely in the present. Their behavior is a series of short-term responses to the environment—reactions to a series of events. Apes are extremely adept at perceiving and registering events. The events they perceive can be complex, have moving parts, clusters of sub-events involving multi-modality patterns of stimuli—all registered as a unit. Yet, they are registered as specific events in time and space, discrete circumstances. Responses are to events. The meaning of an event can only be recalled as a situation-specific event. Apes are unable to re-present events for reflection.

Humans have evolved a general capacity for cultural innovation, opening a formidable gap with the cultures of apes. The cultures of various early hominid cultures have been examined and interpreted as indicating intermediate phases of neuronal representation. These phases, consistent with evolution theory and the self-organizing character of CASs, are preserved as elements in the systems active within us today.

Neuronal representation—Phase 1

The first phase shift occurred about two million years ago. *Homo erectus* is given the credit. Three significant cultural developments by *Homo erectus*—sophisticated community collaboration, consistent management of food, and extensive tool-making—in whatever order they occurred, taken together, are convincing evidence of a qualitative change in mind. These innovations were not simply extensions of cultural characteristics of the apes. A unique neuronal process was required—a capacity for comparing two or more simultaneously present neuronal patterns, a capacity for re-presenting and reflecting on the experience of 'me.' These representations were rehearsable, self-representations built upon knowledge of events.

In this phase, there were significant changes in the processes of intelligence—how registrations, resonance, feedback, and recognition were organized toward a response. *If, then,* and *or* all took on more sophisticated construction. Acquired residual patterns responded to intent *and distinguished the representation of the event from the actual event itself.* The thought of the event, the imagined event, was distinguishable from the actual event.

These innovations depended on a more enhanced neuronal body map, a more distinct calibration of what is happening to me at what part of me. Parts of self and the environment were differentiated and self-represented, comparing two visual representations simultaneously. There were accompanying improvements in: visual motor controls; feedback on the position, motion, and condition of the body; and control of the body's directed action—manual dexterity. Growth in the size of the brain served to increase neuronal capacity and supported the self-organizing adaptation of systems distributed throughout modules of the brain.

Nevertheless, this mind was limited in scope, slow to adapt and restricted in subject matter integration. It was not a symbol-capable mind. Perhaps the greatest achievement of this phase shift was the introduction of *the collective structuring of hominid culture itself.*

Neuronal representation—Phase 2

Cultural evidence for the second phase shift does not appear until the arrival of *Homo sapiens*: a capacity for modeling a series of events across time and space as a continuum of experience and interpretation; and a capacity for representing these models with symbols. These processes of representation operate across episodes. They are metaphorical, deriving general principles and themes across modalities and functional patterns of experience using feedback, resonance, and recognition. This mind could engage in causal explanations, prediction, and control.

The emergence of language was integral to this innovation, and perhaps a marker of something even more profound. In early Stone Age cultures, language was used for the invention of stories—a collectively held, unified set of explanations and metaphors integrating a variety of events in a temporal and causal framework. The appearance of these stories indicates the use of symbolic models of the human experience—efforts to connect smaller-scale events. The use of these stories was contingent upon symbolic invention. Systems of language provided a basis for developing and rehearsing narratives of events, explaining the experiences of the world around us, and inventing narratives that integrate our experiences into a whole—a coherent image of the group and its relationship with the world. Language became the symbolic representation of our experiences.

Neuronal representation—Phase 3

The third phase transition, beginning about 40–50,000 years ago, is most pertinent to our story. The evidence of this transition is manifested in three capacities previously underdeveloped or absent: visual symbols, external memory, and theory construction—a move away from the natural world into a mind-made environment. This capacity is still accelerating.

Visual symbols signaled an important shift in modality from auditory to visual representation, and to an entirely new class of symbols from those used in earlier oral cultures. External memory opened up adjacent possibilities totally finessing the limitations of biological memory. Theory construction demonstrated a capacity for explaining and integrating that, when combined with visual symbols and external memory, provided the means for mind to reflect, refine, and revise on a time scale that extended beyond the life span of a single individual.

This transition also marks two important developments for our story and catalyzes another. The evolution of vision through countless adjacent possibilities was re-energized as the dominant sensory modality. Most importantly, the systems giving rise to the emergence of mind were no longer limited to 'me.' They now extended to systems outside the boundary of me. Mind emerged from me, and the external memory of visual symbols. Last, these changes placed a premium on post-birth development.

The evidence of this last transition is well covered in numerous analyses and publications in several disciplines. Some are noted in the suggested additional reading.

The Rise of the Versatile Mind

In Chapter 5 we noted that the brain's size increased by a factor of three in only 2 million years, an extraordinary growth rate by evolutionary standards. But our bodies did not grow nearly as much. As a consequence the ratio of our brain to body weight is *8 times* that of primitive primates. This larger brain comes with a cost: it consumes 20% of the body's energy and required a reconfiguration of our cranial infrastructure to keep it cool. It is during this 2 million years that many scientists believe we introduced meat into our diet, a source of food that is high in energy. Animals normally evolve no more than is necessary for survival in their environment. During a difficult time in Earth's and our own ancestors' history, with the climate seemingly chaotic, we seem to have spent heavily on unnecessary improvements! Why??

One theory is that the mind became more versatile as a consequence of the rapid climate change and that growth in the size of the brain supported that increase in the versatility of the mind. We saw in Chapter 5 that this enormous growth in the brain coincided with an era during which the climate varied markedly: too fast for physical adaptation by the body. Increased capacity—particularly in the neo-cortex—would have been advantageous to survival: increased capacity for registering, evaluating and anticipating, planning and reacting to the rapidly changing environment. The record available and discussed in other parts of this book indicates this was a period of time when the mind, slowly at first, but inexorably, began to use the environment for its own advantage—setting the stage for our own manufacturing of the environment for our own ends. The mind has progressed from making tools from the environment to making the cyberous environment itself.

What was the connection between the rapid change in climate and the change in the mind and the enormous growth in the brain? It appears that the rapid growth in the brain was simply a by-product of self-organizing CASs moving through adjacent possibilities under the stress caused by the environment. The larger brain was a consequence of population crashes and subsequent population booms! Yet, that increase supported greater versatility in the mind in response to the environment.

Science has used several techniques to measure changes in the Earth's climate over epochs of geological time. Beginning about 25 million years ago, toward the end of the Earth's Oligocene epoch, the slow back and forth changes in climate began to accelerate. During the last 2.5 million years, the climate changes became frenetic by geological and evolutionary standards. There were major climate changes about every 10,000 years and centuries-long fluctuations within the major changes. Significant changes could take place in as little as a decade. They could also flip in as little as three years.

It was not just temperature that changed. Sea levels rose and fell, bringing changes in rain and wind. As moisture was sucked out of the atmosphere, rainfall disappeared, bringing dryness, high winds, severe dust storms, and haze-producing fires. Temperate zones disappeared in sudden droughts and reappeared in sudden resurgence. Vegetation retreated up mountains and then returned. Woodlands became fragmented, transformed into savannah, and then returned. Grasslands and forests, deserts and swamps, traded places. It was a time filled with adjacent possibilities, but the pace was too rapid for the conservative pace of human physical adaptation.

A mind that could function in a variety of different, rapidly changing climates would be advantageous to survival. The time scale of physical evolution could not accommodate the rapid climate changes of that period. The repeated self-organizing of neural systems interacting with one weather extreme after another could lead to the emergence of whole new systems. I want to explore this in more detail.

These climate cycles brought population bottlenecks—crashing populations under stress on one side, and boom times on the other. Survivors with the right stuff thrived when times turned good and hung on when they were bad. Versatile behavior became valuable to survival—species depending on behavioral improvisations would flourish.

These crashes in population left small, isolated groups contending with numerous challenges and opportunities, spread around a landscape that was distressed as well—presenting an abundance of adjacent possibilities. These small groups, unimpeded by the momentum of large populations, were perfect for experimentation—for testing adjacent possibilities.

These natural processes were stimulating hominid systems into adjacent possibilities where some characteristics were useful while others were not. The adjacent possibilities favored some characteristics while suppressing others. Then new adjacent possibilities would favor those previously suppressed and suppress those previously favored—over and over, in step with the whip-lashing changes in climate. The mind was in a constant state of fine-tuning. The right stuff was in constant flux. The result was the emergence of a mind capable of altering behavior in the face of changing conditions, one that could anticipate those changes: a mind with its versatility supported by a brain that had grown by a factor of three.

During this period there seems to have been little or no change in the basic structure of the brain. There were no new modules tacked onto the human neuroanatomy, nothing that the great apes lack. It just got bigger. The increased size likely facilitated the intense increase in interconnectedness that distinguishes the human brain from the brains of other primates... and gives emergence to the mind we have today.

Hominids cruised the edge of chaos. Cohesive populations in stable environments suddenly crashed and splintered. Isolated, splintered groups found opportunities favoring their abilities, and flourished without the competitive momentum of a larger group. Opportunities for experimentation and invention were ample. Sequence and cycling of initial conditions were important to this flow of opportunities and development. Hominids were at the right place at the right time with the right stuff to explore the adjacent possibilities as they opened.

There was a price for this versatility, or perhaps a bonus. During this ride along the edge of chaos the slowing of development during gestation, in deference to the limitations of the birth canal, shifted the heavy work of nurturing from the womb to the group. The birth to weaning phase of life became a central focus of the group. Hominids became the extended keepers and guardians of their feeble infants. Post-birth development moved to an extreme dimension among hominids, extracting a heavy investment in relatively few offspring having slower growth, delayed sexual maturity, and longer life spans. Less obviously, but more importantly, the focus on a lean, mean, physical evolution shifted to opportunistic survival learned in a lengthening post-birth development nurtured by the relationships and knowledge of the members of the group. This was the dawning of the jack-of-all-trades. A species that seldom found a niche it didn't like, molded and adapted environmental niches to the needs of the group.

It was time to stop defining this species by physiological characteristics. The significant initial conditions had become neuronal, networking capacities, not physical ones.

The Anomaly of Mind and Self

Where is that stable core of self? There is none! The self is a dynamic reference: *the residual state, at any given time*, of a continuously self-organizing nervous system interacting with the environment to which it is exposed, incorporating body states over time. It is cumulative experience—up to date. This continuous self-organizing is learning. The self is an inextricable element of the CAS underlying the emergence of mind. Let's unpack that.

As we noted earlier, self-organizing patterns in the brain include those registrations stimulated by the condition of the body. The mind emerging from the brain emerges from patterns that include the condition of the body. The mind builds upon, and includes, the self-referential body state—what's going on in me, my condition at *this* time. Each change in the mind incorporates and reinforces the most primitive aspect of the neuronal CASs—the differentiation between 'me' and 'not me'. What is inside the boundary that is 'me' belongs and what is outside does not. The very essence of meaning is to the *self*. To '*me*.'

There has been an increasingly intense self-referential focus, on 'me,' even as the mind incorporates external storage, depends on technological representation, and increases interaction with extra-body systems. Even as the mind is reaching out to encompass ever more external systems, there is a growing component of self-reference emerging. The importance of what is inside the boundary is increasing. Our preoccupation with me is at an all-time high. We have whole professions of clinicians whose sole purpose is to tend the self—'me. '

This intensifying inclusion of the systems of 'me' and my experience with the environment continues today, even as mind increases its reliance on systems *outside* the boundaries of 'me.' What is happening to meaning… to me? We will explore this in subsequent chapters, particularly while we explore futures of the mind.

Missing in Action and Other Issues of Mind

It is time to begin re-perceiving the mind and the terms we use to describe various aspects of the mind.

Mind is a diaspora of emergence arising from a mashup of CASs, yet we feel whole. We feel like one person, me. We do not feel as if we are a jumbled mish-mash. We don't normally feel as if we are multiple personalities. There is no isolation of the parts. And yet, as we saw in Chapter 5, the brain and the mind emerging from it can fail in ways that indicate neither the brain nor the mind is unified! Yet we might feel that the mind, emerging from whatever parts of the brain are functioning, is unified.

Our mind is experienced through the processes of consciousness: the *current state of interaction* between the human nervous systems and the environment, or *interaction* within the human nervous system—our simulations of the environment—and a combination of the two. There are several aspects of mind of interest here.

First, where is the mind? A multitude of research has focused on various CASs of the brain. Specific parts of the brain consistently affect specific capabilities of the mind. Partial damage to the CASs of the brain leads to changes in the behavior of the mind. Yet, even that is at times only temporary. The plasticity of the self-organizing and the brain's apparent robust organization—with widely dispersed responsibility for functions—lend the brain and emergent mind graceful failure. No single location in the brain is responsible for the mind.

Other research relates observed neuronal activity with specific occupations of the mind—thinking of grandmother, for example. Has this research identified mind in action, or the elements giving rise to mind? Suppose you attend a symphony orchestra performance. You have a wonderful box seat enabling you to watch the actions of all the musicians: the motions of the string sections, the timpani, the woodwinds, and the brass. But your box is soundproof. You hear nothing. At the conclusion of the concert, have you experienced the music? Where was the music during the concert? Was it in the motions of the musicians?

There is also much discussion of the mind's unity. Is the mind unified? Well, maybe it is and maybe it isn't. From instant to instant, the CASs enabling the mind are in constant motion, responding to environmental stimuli… seeking that next adjacent possibility. An emergent mind of the present, unified now—or perhaps a mashup of convenience—is already in transition—as CASs shift beneath its feet.

Does the mind engage in the collaboration of its components? Emergent properties of systems are themselves elements for self-organization without direction. The operations of the vast subterranean agglomeration of sub-systems laboring in the hierarchy—all giving emergence to mind—are not traceable 'causes' of the emergence. The hierarchies of elements, patterns, and self-organizations giving rise to the mind are unknowable to the emergent mind. The components of mind self-organize without direction by the mind. The mind is a consequence not an objective.

Embodied knowledge is the essence of mind. The CASs of the central nervous system respond to environmental stimuli. Inherent in their self-organization is the consequence of the stimulation. The stimuli alter the relationships of the CAS's elements. The next response to stimulus will begin with the residual patterns of the last encounter. The neuronal patterns comprising the CAS and its emergence have learned from the last encounter. They have embodied the experience.

Finally, what is cognition? Cognition is the coalescence of all the self-organizing patterns involved in receiving, storing, and processing disturbances—the operation of perception, recognition, learning, and response. It is the effecting of *if-then react thus… or* based on experience with stimuli, react in another manner.

Whatever the perspective of the changing mind, a dance of complex adaptive systems began eons ago—ultimately including systems studied today as neurological, sociological, psychological, cultural, cognitive, linguistic, or cybernetic—a dance that continues to sweep us along into the future of the mind.

Suggested Additional Reading for Chapter 8

The evolution of the mind has been explored from three perspectives. Steven Mithen's *The Pre-History of the Mind* discusses the mind's progression through three major reorganizations over 55,000 millennia. Merlin Donald's *Origins of the Modern Mind* examines the changes in the processes of representation in mind. William Calvin's *The Ascent of Mind* examines the forces influencing the increasing versatility of mind.

Jonathan Lunine, in *Earth: Evolution of a Habitable World,* provides an extensive discussion of the earth's environment in which our minds evolved, including an analysis of the climate changes of the last 2 million years.

Terrence Deacon, in *Incomplete Nature: How Mind emerged from Matter*, provides a re-perception of mind, consciousness and self. Douglas Hofstadter, in *I Am A Strange Loop*, explores a re-perception of consciousness and 'self.' Traditional concepts of mind have been explored from other perspectives and with conflicting theories. A few are mentioned here. Ray Jackendoff explores the mind from a computational perspective in *Consciousness and the Computational Mind.* Both Marvin Minsky in *The Society of Mind,* and Stephen Pinker, in *How the Mind Works*, explore a mind composed of collaborating sub-minds. Annette Karmiloff-Smith, in *Beyond Modularity: A Developmental Perspective on Cognitive Science*, explores a process for the mind's continuing reorganization and the consequent emergent property. Daniel Dennett, in *Consciousness Explained*, provides a provocative discussion of consciousness.

The relationship of mind and body has been explored from several perspectives, including Francisco Varela *et al* in *The Embodied Mind: Cognitive Science and Human Experience.* Nicholas Humphrey discusses the relationship of mind to body and the emergence of self, in *A History of the Mind.* Raymond Gibbs, in *Embodiment and Cognitive Science*, provides a broader exploration of the mind-body relationship. Antonio Damasio's books noted previously and based on clinical research, explore the mind's embodiment of physical experience. George Lakoff and Mark Johnson in *Metaphors We Live By* develop the relationships of experience, categorization, metaphor, cognition, and mind.

Stuart Kauffman's *At Home in the Universe* explores that first ratcheting-up of CASs into life... and our inevitability. *Emergence: Contemporary Readings in Philosophy and Science*, edited by Mark Bedau and Paul Humphreys includes essays addressing the hierarchical nature of CASs and emergence.

PART THREE

Interfaces, Post-Birth Development, and Augmentation

In Part Three we trace the increasing importance of the third force in the future of the mind. Post-birth development, made possible by ever more sophisticated interfaces, has blossomed in the cyberous world of sensuous augmentation. Our attention has been siphoned away from the disturbances of nature toward abstract disturbances of our own making. It is as if our meditative gaze into our navel has become an end in itself.

As we have ambled through the adjacent possibilities of sensuous augmentation exposed by the initial conditions of post-birth development and culture, we have focused on the patterns of earlier minds. Passage through a countless sequence of initial conditions and adjacent possibilities over the last 40 thousand years has accelerated our collaboration with, and our control of, "what is happening out there."

We now focus on the self-organizing patterns within silicon-based systems—those electronic augmentations in our environment—and what those self-organizing patterns represent, uniquely to us. More than any other interface, this collaboration with the synthetic systems augmenting vision has changed the nature of our sensuous transactions and registrations with "what is happening out there." The intensification of intimacy with the cyberous representations of "what is happening out there" increasingly blurs into "what is happening to me." These relationships, these self-organizing collaborations with the synthetic environment, expose the mind to new adjacent possibilities.

The sounds of mind are being uprooted by the sights of mind at an accelerating pace; visual concepts are increasingly supplementing words. Neuronal registration, self-organizing, recognition, and response to disturbances of sight are relentlessly prodding metaphor and cognition. Environmental elements we design to provoke sight encompass the words of sounds of mind in a visual language—supplementing the very concepts represented by the sounds of words. Windows' vibrating hourglass and Google's spinning arrow, among the more familiar, beg our patience...

wordlessly. The mind is in revolution, in a phase shift seizing cognition from the sounds of mind for the sights of mind.

Yet, nothing physically new is required of our bodies. No physical change is needed, although we should expect some moves into adjacent neuronal possibilities that enhance collaboration with the cyberous culture we have produced. It is simply a matter of honing the serendipitous, collaborative self-organization among elements of the central nervous systems and elements of the cyberous environment.

In Part Three, we will explore the expansion of the neuronal registrations—of self-organizations, the resonances of pattern recognition, and the responses of *if-then... or*—to the incorporation of environments constructed by the very 'selfs' affected. We will explore the cyberous augmentation of our very 'selfs'. We design these augmentations to be supple extensions of our own sensuous interfaces. They are powerful influences on the self-organizing and the residual patterns of our neuronal systems—our 'selfs'.

We will examine culture as an incubator for the force of post-birth development—the postponement of maturity in the interest of self-organization of the mind. We will consider the implications for post-birth development and for that self-organization, the implications of weaning the sensuous interfaces from disturbances of the physical, natural environment, focusing them instead on our own self-made, cyberous disturbances.

Part Three will prepare us to consider the future of the mind in a world of post-birth development incubated by a cyberous culture of our own making.

CHAPTER 9
The Sensuous Interfaces

The San Francisco-Oakland Bay Bridge is a sprawling tangle of concrete and steel working around, over, and through a teeming ant hill of people and their accoutrements. The bridge is an interface. It connects two distinct areas—San Francisco on one side, Oakland, Emeryville, and Berkeley on the other. Each area is a functioning system in its own right. The interface enables an exchange between the two areas—people and vehicles. On one side there are multiple interstate and surface street approaches and exits integrated by 'spaghetti junction.' On the other side is a similar tangle of cement and signs.

Interfaces are all around us and in us, at all imaginable scales, from bridges, to our respiratory system, to the synapses of neurons. Our five senses are interfaces with the environment. So is that screen you look at all day. So is the mouse and the touch-screen. We are going to explore our sensuous interfaces because they are important to our ever increasing relationship with the cyberous environment. Our sensuous interfaces have a trajectory of their own within our culture.

This chapter is itself an interface.

First, it is an interface between the human and the extra-human nature of our story. So far in our story we have emphasized the nature of humans— that familiar part we can examine physically. Much of the study of the evolution of humans is cemented to physical evidence—fossils and the artifacts we find among them. We have focused on physical boundaries and physical interfaces, too. In this chapter we begin exploring the extra-physical and extra-physical boundaries.

Secondly, this chapter is an interface between, on the one hand, the first two parts of the book, in which principally the physical phenomena important to our story have been explored, and, on the other hand, the remainder of the book, in which we will explore those nonphysical phenomena that arise out of the interaction of the physical ones.

In this chapter we explore five stages of the continuing increase in the complexity of interfaces and interaction between humans as biological systems: verbalization and orality; images and art; writing and print, which are distinct but will be explored together; and electronic technologies and cyberous interfaces. A sixth, culture, is also an interface but, as the incubator of post-birth development, it warrants a discussion of its own. We will explore culture in the next chapter. More importantly, we will explore the increase in the complexity of interfaces and collaborations between human systems and the nonbiological, synthetic systems in the environment. We will do this by examining the properties arising from the interaction of these internal and external systems with one another. We will also examine the increased complexity and sophistication required within humans to support these interfaces and interactions.

Third, our exploration of collaborations, exchanges, and interfaces among CASs will address those not requiring a near physical proximity—interactions with disturbances remote in both time and space. The interfaces required for these self-organizations are becoming increasingly sophisticated and are encountered increasingly early in life. These factors serve to intensify post-birth development.

But first, what are interfaces? How are they important? And what is their relevance to this story?

Interfaces

An interface is where two systems exchange something. Back to the bridge. Where does the bridge begin? A simple question—where is the bridge? Where is the interface? The answer is not so simple. Interfaces have supporting structures that may extend far into the systems connected. Surface streets are modified to facilitate approaches to the bridge beginning blocks away with dedicated street lanes. Are these parts of the bridge? What of the synchronized traffic lights facilitating the smooth exchange with the bridge? What of street crossings forbidding pedestrian traffic in order to facilitate vehicular traffic approaching the bridge? Is this constraint part of the bridge? What of the signage and the lighting directing vehicles to the bridge? Does the bridge begin where drivers begin adjusting for the encounter with the intersections that lead to the bridge? Or is it where drivers begin considering what they must do to enter the bridge—or perhaps avoid congestion caused by the bridge? Does the bridge include that moment when a driver, still backing out of the driveway, begins anticipating the encounter with the traffic congestion caused by the bridge?

This terminological difficulty grows with the complexity of the systems served by the interface, the complexity of the exchange between systems, and dynamic accommodation of fluctuating exchange. As interfaces evolved for more complex exchanges, the demarcations between systems became increasingly dynamic and amorphous. Interfaces reached deeper into systems on each side of the boundary as each system self-organized to support exchanges—assembly, shaping, parsing, interpreting, and responding. We may well wonder where the bridge begins and ends.

Interfaces are integral to Complex Adaptive Systems. Elements of CASs establish exchanges through interfaces. Each participant in the CAS must support interface activities with preparation and assimilation. It is not always obvious where an interface begins and ends. As systems and their exchanges grew in sophistication so did interfaces. The preparation and assimilation of interfaces extend throughout CASs, coalescing into the very elements they support.

Our sensuous interfaces support exchanges with the environment, integrating "what's happening to me?" with "what's happening out there?" Hominid interfaces have self-organized to facilitate increasingly sophisticated interaction with external systems. We will consider the properties arising from these interactions, the increased sophistication required to support them, and the phase shifts which changed the proximity of interaction from near to remote.

Setting the Stage—Multicellular, Multifunctional Organisms

There is a tendency in science and among the general public to perceive change in the context of our own species' brief time of existence. As we have seen with pattern recognition and vision, the stage on which we are only newcomers extends millions of years into the past. Setting the stage, exploring the development of natural interfaces before our species' time, will improve our understanding of the commonality we have with the eons-long development of natural interfaces *and* the unique relationship our species has developed with artificial, synthetic interfaces of our own design.

Each CAS and each basic element of each CAS needs interfaces: on-off ramps, traffic control systems, and signage to support and facilitate the exchanges between elements within the CAS and exchanges of the CAS with the environment. At first, multi-cellular organisms were simple: registration of disturbances—information—and reactions to that information. As the complexity of exchange increased, so did the supporting infrastructure on each side of the interfaces.

More information is an advantage—and nature rides a winner. A whole stream of initial conditions and adjacent possibilities in successive hierarchies of collaboration banded together to perform even more multiple functions to the advantage of the whole. There was an explosion of life forms as information about the environment moved through the interfaces into the very bowels of the organisms. Today, hominids have an almost incomprehensibly complex set of interfaces among our systems and our environment. That includes the interfaces we use with each other.

The raw material and the supporting infrastructure we have for interacting within ourselves, and with the environment is formidable. We have explored these systems in previous chapters. All of them have exchanges across these boundaries and each element has a supporting structure for the exchange. The smell of a rose may seem simple in its pleasing quality, yet hundreds if not thousands of interfaces work to bring us the sensation—sensuous interfaces.

We begin our exploration of these sensuous interfaces unique to humans with speech and language.

Verbalization and Orality

These interfaces enable the transfer of information between individuals, fostering learning and knowledge among members sharing a common language environment. Generally, interest has been centered on the development and use of language. Yet, it is the quality of being oral, the systems underlying the ability to verbalize, that is the nexus of the interface. In the context of the interface, language arises from that set of systems supporting information preparation and assimilation—whatever else its component systems may be as they participate in other systems.

Language was an early interface for information exchange among CASs. It was the product of a remarkable and profound phase transition in the numerous systems giving rise to the interface. Nevertheless, it is limiting. Consider:

- A spoken-only language has 2–3,000 words, and no history of those words.

- Spoken words are transitional with no visual presence, place, or duration—they disappear immediately.

- Knowledge carried by spoken words is confined to the location of the knower and sharing requires a relationship with the knower.

- Knowledge is stored with community energy through the repetition of patterns in speeches and stories.

- In oral societies, spoken words only represent the experiences of life... not ideas.

- If spoken words lose their continuing relevance to life and are not used, they disappear along with the knowledge they convey.

Even today, the oral tradition, though an enormous advance over pre-oral species, inhibits actions we take for granted. "Look it up" is meaningless— there is no place to look; research is experiential and difficult to share; innovation is practice; and abstraction is inexpressible. Most importantly, these interfaces limit the raw material available, the processes, structure, recall, and the basis for sharing... thought! Today, our own pre-literate children experience an oral culture.

Finally, this interface is exclusive, if you don't know the language, you don't know.

Images and Art

These appeared about 50,000–100,000 years ago. Early cultures depended on the visual interpretation of facial expressions. Visual neuronal systems many times richer in resources and more extensively interconnected than any other, probably coupled with the dexterity imbued by a million years of tool-making, set the stage for this adjacent possibility. Hominids passed through a phase shift that opened into adjacent possibilities we are still exploring. Importantly, humans began augmenting their internal systems with external ones.

There were profound consequences.

- Sensory registrations shifted from nature to human-made patterns.

- Manifestations of personal imagination persisted after the artist.

- Representations were possible without a witness.

- The integration and interaction of human and synthetic systems began.

- The nature of orality and verbalization—exclusion—was mitigated by images that transcend language.

Producing the image of a thought requires a remarkable collaboration among neuronal subsystems. The brain's elements began collaborating across functional capabilities. Using visual images involves: planning and executing preconceived mental patterns; an intention to communicate some displaced set of patterns; and attributing meaning to synthetic visual patterns—an image not part of its referent.

The implications of this phase shift are enormous and continue today. This interface enables:

- The separation of observation from observer.

- The separation of knowledge from knower.

- The means for projecting whole concepts and ideas from individuals *into* the environment, for independent use by other individuals.

Most importantly, humans began designing both interfaces and external systems for adjacent possibilities open uniquely to them. Humans began shaping their own adjacent possibilities—creating stimuli that would prompt their own self-organization.

Writing and Print

These two interfaces further advanced the separation of observations, ideas, and experiences from the individual of origin.

Writing appeared about 5,000 years ago. It continued the severance of humans from their natural environment begun by verbalization: of place and time from individual observation, and concept from personal experience. It enabled information transfer independent of person or environment, and learning beyond apprenticeship.

Writing accelerated the divergence of culture from nature by enabling abstraction of time and location—an interface with the notion of pure and featureless space—perhaps more real to us today than the world we live in.

Writing gave ideas a life of their own, independent from the natural environment, from the experience of individuals or groups. Contrasted with oral cultures, writing left physical residues. Writing left ideas and thoughts in the environment for reproduction and endless sharing. Writing encouraged a critical review of words in private, abstract classification and examination of phenomena and hypotheses, remote from the origin. The self could interact with its own verbalizations made physical, ponder those statements, and relate with itself in isolation.

Writing introduced two paradoxes:

First, writing represents sounds, written words. Writing must ultimately be related to sound for meaning. The sounds in turn represent experience and concepts; they have patterns of organization easily shared among CASs of the brain; and they support the emergence of the mind we know so well. Writing needs the sounds of oral language, but oral language does not need writing. The sequences of hierarchical formation and emergence in CASs do make a difference.

Second, writing inextricably ties sounds into a visual field—a visual link to spoken words, to sounds. Reading is interacting with sounds on a surface. Visual sounds became part of the visible world—focusing visual registration on marks representing sounds—giving sound a visual presence.

Print also introduced two additional dimensions for abstraction. Print, playing to the needs of the preparation and assimilation of human CAS interfaces, synthetically shapes the environment for consumption by the CAS. A table of contents is for the reader, not of the sounds of the producer. Print implies accuracy and completeness. Dictionaries cite 'correct' meaning and pronunciation. Yet, sounds, with their preceding initial conditions subtly extending throughout the central nervous system, remain a powerful transporter of ideas and a basis for metaphor. Writing and print strengthened the influence of culture during post-birth self-organization.

This interaction of oral words and visible words as external artifacts of ourselves, demonstrates the persistent, pervasive interfaces between those CASs comprising what we are. Initial conditions *do* matter. This interface prepared us for the increasing influence of synthetic systems participating with our own—through interfaces that we ourselves develop.

Electronic Technologies and Cyberous Interfaces

These interfaces enable instant broadcast and knowledge-sharing in real or shifted time, interactions among limitless CASs in any location, with multiple environments... including both ourselves and machines.

Three aspects of these interfaces are important:

1. They intensify interaction between and with their creators. The supple feedback between neuronal and synthetic systems is inseparable from the systems themselves. Where does the bridge begin and end?

2. They enable interactions between abstractions in non-physical environments, between ourselves and our abstractions, and between abstractions alone. We write programs in print. They pass through interfaces and translations, are reduced to 1s and 0s, and ultimately are represented by electron patterns in silicon. These patterns self-organize and interact according to simple rules, manifest themselves back to 1s and 0s and ultimately to images. The visual images of the Graphic User Interface augment print. Neuronal systems are increasingly self-organizing in response to the disturbances of electronic interfaces prompted by the self-organizing electron patterns in silicon.

3. These interfaces make possible CASs that are comprised of both our own neuronal systems and our synthetic creations.

The mobility of our cyberous interfaces is special. Mobility is a game changer and requires additional comment.

1. Desktop connections require you to be at the desk in order to connect and interact. It may be a Personal Computer, but it is confined to its installed location. Not even notebook computers are always or conveniently available for interaction. These are not a readily/always available interface. It is not really personal. It is mine but not me. Mobility takes these interfaces off the desk and puts them in our pockets where they are always available. They are as much a part of our lives as are the flesh and blood in our neuronal systems in our heads.

2. An interface that is with me all the time, is part of me. Whenever I want to interact, it is there! It is at my service just like my senses!

3. Mobility extends vision. If I see an event down the street, it stimulates my neurons; they self-organize and become part of my residual self. So now, a friend, or someone friended, sends me a video from a mobile device, how do my neurons distinguish the two? Vision is the collaboration of the systems of sight with other CASs!

4. Embodied knowledge: the self-organized neurons are an embodiment of my visual experience. My smartphone provides an extension of what I see, an extension of that visual experience, of what is embodied in the self-organization of my neurons wherever I am. It is with me as a pervasive, continuing sensor/interface extending beyond the limits of my sensuous interfaces wherever I am—it is with me. It is not a stretch to say it is of me, perhaps even... me!

The immediacy and inclusiveness of these systems are without parallel. They open adjacent possibilities that were unthinkable only a decade ago. We will expand on the implications of this mobility in Part Four of the book.

Our electromagnetic interfaces, promoted by our culture and encapsulating post-birth development, easing into adjacent possibilities with us, have thrust us into a metamorphosis that is both thrilling and chilling. Vision is finessing the bounds of sound. Vision is the most sophisticated sensuous interface by far. Photography, movies, and television extend visual interfaces first opened by images and art. The web is accelerating this move into the visual. Now images come to us—in the forms we want, when we want. Vision is asserting dominance.

The body may still lay claim to the physical self and the subjective present, but what of the emergent mind? Where are the boundaries of CASs that enable mind's emergence? Has the synthetic augmentation of the senses extended the boundaries of the CASs that are me? Does the synthetic augmentation evolve, too? Where does the bridge begin? Where does it end? Before we consider the possibilities we need to explore two more issues: culture and post-birth development.

Suggested Additional Reading for Chapter 9

Walter Ong's *Orality and Literacy* traces the transition from oral to literate cultures and the influence of these different interfaces on thinking, including learning from electronic sources. David Abram considers the downside of this transition in *The Spell of the Sensuous* suggesting that the introduction of writing initiated our disengagement from the natural sensuous world.

The integrative nature of interfaces has been influential on the development of the mind. Steven Mithen's *The Prehistory of the Mind: The Cognitive Origins of Art and Science* explores the seamless integration of the elements of mind 50–100,000 years ago, highlighting the gradual unfolding of ever more resourceful interfaces and their importance to an integrated mind. Annette Karmiloff-Smith, in *Beyond Modularity: A Developmental Perspective on Cognitive Science*, explores the neural domains sympathetic to environmental interfaces.

Elaine Morgan, in *The Descent of the Child*, provides perspectives on the learning of language by infants in a culture. Howard Gardner, in *Frames of Mind: the Theory of Multiple Intelligences,* presents the need for all capabilities to be in place and working together in the modern mind and how that mind is pruned by culture during post-birth development. Marshall McLuhan in *The Gutenberg Galaxy* enthralled a whole generation with his descriptions of the transformative interface—the medium is both the message and the massage.

Marc Prensky, in *Don't Bother Me Mom—I'm Learning*, reports on the symbiosis of the 'under thirties' generation with and through the Web.

Jason Farman, in *Mobile Interface Theory: Embodied Space and Locative Media*, explores the transformative nature of mobility and the ever-ready interface with remote 'not me.'

CHAPTER 10
Post-Birth Development and Culture

Post-birth development and culture demonstrate the intimate relationship between 'me' and 'not me.' Post-birth development takes place in 'me.' My neurons develop in consequence of stimulation. My vision learns to recognize what is out there. My systems self-organize in response to stimulation. Post-birth development is all about 'me.' Culture is that most pressing, intimate aspect of 'not me.' Culture provides the most intimate stimulation of 'me.' Yet, the 'me' of post-birth development also influences the 'not me' of culture. Though separate, it is difficult to discuss one without the other.

The development and acquisition of cultural traits, a unique means of adaptation, is an extraordinary aspect of *Homo sapiens's* movement into adjacent possibilities. Our cultural adaptation has allowed us to transform diverse environments while redefining ourselves. The rules, residual patterns of members' interactions, artifacts, and tools of culture, constitute the environment to which infants are exposed, the environment in which children self-organize—initially... and for life!

Culture is a non-genetic form of adaptation. Culture and the artifacts of culture are not inherited. Culture is learned and, in turn, taught. Culture is handed down, generation to generation—outside of genetics. It emerges from a collaboration of individuals yet it is independent of those comprising it. The interactions of this system provide dynamic residual patterns that persist so long as there are elements to interact. So long as there are individuals interacting in accordance with the rules and relationships of the culture, the patterns of the culture will persist.

Culture has several aspects of interest to us. First, culture provides for information transmission: what is learned from the interactive group in which one is born and matures. In this respect it is an interface for its members.

Second it is the emergent property of a community whose members interact according to a set of rules. It is an environment for 'me,' and for elements reacting to 'me.'

Third, culture is a proactively participating member of the systems comprising 'me.' Culture prepares me to live within it, and in turn, my actions can influence its future. My culture interacts with me, provides me the tools and rules for earning a living, and approves or disapproves of me.

Last and most important to this story, it is also the incubator of post-birth development, one of three trajectories into adjacent possibilities leading to the future of the mind. We begin with a broad review of the evolution of culture and explore its relationship with post-birth development—the relationship between 'me' and 'not me.'

The Evolution of Culture

The behavior of individual primates takes place within the context of their bodily structure and sensory registration. But most primates also relate to other primates in groups. Common to most primates is a social structure containing: several generations; a mixed-sex group; a social context for adult members; a means for satisfying hunger; and organizing for procreation, nurturing, and security. It is from this base that our cultural system emerged.

Research indicates there was a steady drift into the adjacent possibilities of group collaboration in the earliest hominids. Science has considered the examples of other primates' collaboration as precursors of early hominid culture. These cultures contain the initial conditions for the emergence of hominid culture. Studies of other primate cultures indicate multiple interactions: friendships, alliances, learning, teaching, security, mating, feeding and nurturing the young—applying collective solutions to most dilemmas of life. Primates are known to expose their young to situations which aid learning and these learned behavior patterns accumulate within groups to form common patterns, or traditions. The long journey through adjacent possibilities has equipped primates with the ability to register disturbances and accumulate knowledge of the environment not simply as individuals, but as a group through the patterns of group interaction.

Apes, for example, actively seek out novel environments and adapt to them with associated behavioral changes. These changes are promoted by the younger ranking individuals of a group. Learning potential seems to be concentrated in the period before puberty and adolescence, perhaps before repeated self-organization of neuronal patterns has established LTP residuals. Yet adults with more interaction experience and repeated residual patterns possess more environmental knowledge for integrating novel facts. We also have the artifacts of early hominid cultures which indicate a slow but persistent move into group collaboration. Analyses of extant hunter-gatherer societies provide insight, too.

Over several million years interacting capabilities developed—each a phase shift in its own right. These both encouraged and relied upon new modes of collaboration, new modes of social organization:

- bipedalism

- freed hands

- estrus in females

- mixed scavenging and foraging

- brain reorganization and growth.

These capabilities seemed to reach a tipping point about 2.5 million years ago. Hominids began making stone tools and began the practice of group congregation at a "home base." Stone tools accompanied the first cooperative subsistence strategy, based on reciprocity and sharing. Tool-making also indicates learning-based forms of group cohesion and interdependence.

Most importantly, tool-making reinforced the influence of hominids on their changing environment, facilitating a group way of life advantageous for adaptation to niches. Hominids began altering that environment for their use—a significant change in the relationship with disturbances in the environment. Adjacent possibilities favoring division of responsibility and division of labor within the group became an advantage for responding to disturbances in the environment. There was a growing value in collaborative adaptation as a way of responding to environmental changes. Culture became self-reinforcing. Collaboration opened a new set of adjacent possibilities for exploring even more collaboration.

It is this collective acquisition and transmission of an accumulation of residual, learned patterns, used as a unique means of adaptation, that is the most extraordinary aspect of the evolution and post-birth development of the genus *Homo*.

The Big Chills and the Big Bang

Environmental stress and self-organization of mind are integral companions to cultural change. Many factors contributed to the emergence of hominids, but—as we have seen—the stress of rapid climate variation characterized the era. The many micro-climates and localized habitats provided diverse, changing, and unreliable food resources. This was an era promoting opportunistic omnivorous foraging of seasonally available food in micro-niches of the environment. The same environmental conditions underlying the emergence of the versatile mind presented possibilities for increased collaboration. There would have been adjacent possibilities for developing carnivorous behavior, if only scavenging, for times and seasons when other high-yielding nutritional sources were not available. It was an era for the dynamic self-organization of individuals with multiple skills into groups with shifting divisions of labor and responsibilities as the opportunities and threats they faced varied by season and migration. It was a time and location for hominid collaboration and cooperative adaptation, favoring the exploration of multiple adjacent possibilities.

Culture changed the terms of change itself. Once a cultural system self-organized, individual and social and environmental factors did not simply interact as one. The elements of each opened still more adjacent possibilities for CAS exploration. As with any CAS, the adjacent possibilities of each element and each level of the hierarchy enrich the adjacent possibilities of the whole. Each of the elements comprising culture—individuals and groups, relationships, artifacts and tools, learning, security—together provide combinations and permutations of adjacent possibilities for the whole. The self-organization of culture as an adaptive strategy was a breakthrough in the history of life. It was the culmination of a long sequence of initial conditions and the exploration of adjacent possibilities. The climate was the straw that stirred the drink.

Four dimensions of culture are of particular interest to post-birth development: a 'home base', division of labor, extended nurturing, and an abstract essence of the community—that which is of the group without belonging exclusively to any individual.

Home Base: Learning, Place, and Community

Group living and child-rearing, with a 'home base', is an integral part of culture and a catalyst for post-birth development—for learning.

Post-birth brain development with extended maturation was an adjacent possibility facilitated by the attributes of culture. The advantages of cultural adaptation became increasingly important to hominids typified by delayed sexual maturity, longer life, and reorganized and enlarged brains. What once might have been discrete adjacent possibilities became continuing processes for learning and communications. Organic and behavioral changes integrated as the elements of both interacted and self-organized together.

Pattern acquisition and recognition by children today—learning—progresses through a definitive series of initial conditions and self-organizations, a sequence that is supported by brain growth and activated by social interaction from birth. As with all self-organizing systems, the initial conditions for each self-organization matter. Whatever patterns become residual form the initial conditions for subsequent acquisitions, for subsequent development. An infant's early interaction with the environment of culture leaves patterns for life.

Children, for instance, seem compelled to accomplish the formidable task of learning speech and later to fully develop their language skills. Yet, for what concepts, for which sounds of mind, for what kind of vocalization, under what rules—which set of syntax and semantics—which language? The initiation of these self-organizations, the acquisition of these patterns, is activated by the surroundings of the place and the activities of the community within it—the culture.

Division of Labor: Foragers, Hunter-Gatherers, and Farmers

A second dimension of culture of interest to us is that the simultaneous, alternative ways of making a living reinforce both the need and the capacity for division of labor, collaboration, and learning. Division of labor opened the exploration of multiple adjacent possibilities by individuals thus contributing to additional adjacent possibilities for the collaborating whole.

The ways our ancestors made a living, the ecological niches they found and increasingly created on their own—is a story important to our own. Our ways of life are incredibly diverse today. It was millions of years ago that our ancestors took the first step toward that diversity—from foraging and scavenging, through hunter-gathering, to farming and manufacturing... and online!

The differences in logistics between gathering and hunting—the acquisition and application of knowledge, planning and preparation, the collaborative execution—would have reinforced a tendency for different skills to become superior in different individuals. This in turn fostered the development of complex, parallel changes in relationships. Social skills would be required for mutual protection from predators, rules for cooperative hunting and dividing food, for division of labor and increased interdependence.

Whether hunting or scavenging, the activity of obtaining and consuming meat had strong social consequences. Hominids had encroached on the niches of carnivores. Learning, rules, agreements, and reciprocal understanding had to underlie a tool-based way of life. As hominids relied more on a combination of technology and social organization, activities such as planning cooperation, division of labor, and accurate mental maps of foraging ranges and migrations to new sources of food would have been important adjacent possibilities to be explored by a mind capable of myriad tasks.

These hominids, living in complex social groups, were the most flexible and intelligent animals of their time. The adjacent possibilities leading to the *Homo* lineage was opened in conjunction with this mental and social complexity—through the interaction of a changing environment and group organization. Internal changes, reacting with ecological change, produced both cultural solutions and new physical forms. Physical forms? Yes, new forms to take advantage of new adjacent possibilities presented by culture: feet supporting erect carriage, long journeys, fight or flight... or a kick into the goal with seconds left; supple hands capable of grasping tools, tearing meat or peeling potatoes, drawing on cave walls, printing text, delicate surgery, or the Mendelssohn violin concerto; topped off by the large central nervous system of the versatile mind.

This ability to be opportunistic under numerous and changing situations offered by both environment and relationships began a long sequence of moves into adjacent possibilities that continues today. Post-birth development takes place in this environment of diversity.

Extended Nurturing

The third dimension of interest is a nurturing one. Culture is a container for Lamarckian adaptation and re-organization by the young. Lamarck

POST-BIRTH DEVELOPMENT AND CULTURE

theorized that skills acquired by individuals were passed on to their descendants, thus accounting for adaptation in evolution. The individual CAS—me—collaborates with other individuals—not me—in a higher level CAS that persists for the benefit of 'me' and also for 'not me'. This self-organizing enables the emergence of 'me', but as part of a culture, a CAS, that transcends 'me'. Individuals outside of us are part of our external environment and we are part of theirs.

Human evolution has become a process of adaptation through culture—of registering and constantly self-organizing into new initial conditions, new residual patterns. Culture initiates processes of development and maturation, provides a reservoir of patterns for learning and structure, and conveys rules, choices, symbols, and understanding for the young. We are inherently gregarious with an urge to communicate—to interact.

As noted earlier, a simple *if-then* system of registration, recognition, and response—typical of short-lived animals—does not allow for modification of behavior by learning. There is little or no parent care. Newborns hit the ground running with largely inherited patterns. Adaptation is genetic. Species with longer periods of parental care have adapted to learning opportunities allowing new information to be acquired through experience. The inclination to learn is predisposed. Restless neuronal systems constantly register patterns of disturbance and reorganize, laying down a stream of residual patterns for resonance—for recognition. Experience and interaction fill in the gaps with details of the contemporary environment. *If-then…. or* systems provide for alternative responses.

Beyond some of our primitive emotions, humans are not hard-wired with set responses to environmental disturbances. Our genetics provide for continuous reorganization in response to environmental disturbances. The process is flexible and highly adaptive, acquiring experiences in contemporary environments. A great diversity of adaptation is possible. Changing environments and new resources are opportunities for new adaptations.

Culture is of inestimable adaptive value for rapid creative changes and innovations. It is highly flexible and capable of diffusion to dispersed populations in less than a single generation. This ability to transmit information and behavior through learning today equips us to explore adjacent possibilities that were unimagined a generation ago.

Members of a culture can arbitrarily impose significance. This unique endowment allows the naming and classifying of objects and the

129

arrangement of an ordered system of concepts. Learned participation in this naming and classifying not only continues significance, it endows membership. Learning a language involves the mastering and interaction of discrimination, mental structures for syntax and meaning, vocabulary and accurate pronunciation. This is a formidable task and yet children appear to enjoy it. Toddlers love naming things.

Learning, the acquisition of patterns, new initial conditions and new residuals for recognition, involves self-organizing of previous experience. Pattern recognitions take place in context, never generalized. Context is both personal and cultural. Speaking, reading and thinking are cultural interactions. A single symbol, book, or experience may be of historical, religious, or literary significance—depending on the context, the place in relationships with others, the place in the environment of culture. This is the behavior of a CAS—elements interacting with other elements in an environment of rules.

Culture is a protocol for interaction, for transactions with other individuals through our sensuous interfaces. The relationship of group living and child rearing is an integral part of culture—and an extremely strong catalyst for the self-organization of learning. It is also a strong influence on available adjacent possibilities. The long duration of human immaturity allows children to self-organize within an increasingly complex environment. Infants, incipient CASs, absorb disturbances and self-organize residual patterns—learning from experiences, from their environment. The rules of interaction—residual patterns of members' interactions, artifacts, and tools—constitute the environment to which infants are exposed. Culture is the environment in which a child self-organizes. This post-birth development is a strong influence on moves into adjacent possibilities of the mind. It is one of the three eons-long evolutionary trajectories shaping the future of the mind. An important aspect of this post-birth development is the visual influence of the environment of culture.

Abstract Essence of The Community: Art, Science, and Religion

The fourth important dimension of culture is the interaction of the communal 'abstract'—that which is of the group without belonging exclusively to any individual—with the rise of self-consciousness, and self-reflection that prepared us for machine interaction.

There are various explanations and observations on the appearance of art in the artifacts of *Homo sapiens*. Whether as communicating or defining adornment, worship of the unknown, or record of experience, biological evolution will not explain this phenomenon. After the emergence of cave art, striking in its complete conceptual presentation, in its sudden leap into the representational abstract, the disturbances of the environment would never be the same.

The use of foreign materials in the sudden appearance of ornaments also indicates a novel form of self-definition, of self-consciousness that emerged with an external mode of social display. The high value accorded to nonessential items such as an ornate staff or a bracelet indicates a profound change in social relations—perhaps a shift toward the participation of not just 'me,' but of whole groups of 'me,' an indication of aggregations indicating membership in 'not me,' the emergence of group identity. Here were the elements of a newly self-organizing CAS.

But why did this capacity arise about 35,000 years ago? What processes resulted in this sudden need for social display? Perhaps the decorative body was first used as a symbolic stage to enact new divisions in society—ranking systems—and as a way for individuals to demonstrate distinctiveness. If so, art may have first arisen to fulfill social and psychological needs associated with everyday forms of group interaction—interfaces facilitating the self-organizing elements of the heretofore distinct and individual 'me.'

Cultural context is required to give meaning to representation: a baby's babble will not lead to language without a cultural context. Marks will not be symbols outside a socially supported symbolic system. Feedback is required between the individuals in a group and the ongoing cultural structure. There must be context for information exchange. Information has a social life!

The elements were in place. The adjacent possibilities were there. The time had come. The emergence and development of art was the consequence of a series of interconnected relational and environmental changes interacting and exploring adjacent possibilities from a set of initial conditions. It was the beginning of a punctuation in the equilibrium of the time, a phase shift that still encompasses us today. It was a step into the adjacent possibilities of visual thinking and visual language.

Before exploring the continuing influence of culture and post-birth development in the cyber age, we will consider in more detail these two aspects of culture: visual thinking and visual language.

Suggested Additional Reading for Chapter 10

John Odling-Smee, *et al*, in *Niche Construction: the Neglected Process in Evolution*, lay the groundwork for the importance of culture as a knowledge transmitting vehicle active in adaptation. In his introduction to *Autopoiesis and Cognition*, Humberto Maturana explores societies as phenomenal domains in the context of autopoiesis, the relationships of societies, their components, and the properties of their components. Donald Michael, in *With Both Feet Planted in Mid-Air*, an essay in *In Search of the Missing Elephant*, elaborates on the fragmented, incoherent, and unpredictable nature of emergent society; while, in *Learning to Plan and Planning to Learn,* he explores learning by society itself, and the need for understanding and toleration in the processes of societal learning.

Tim Megarry, in *Society in Prehistory*, investigates the early stages of hominid culture, and William Calvin, in *The Ascent of Mind*, discusses the influence of rapid climate change on hominids. The complex interactions within cultures are the subject of Lee Cronk's *That Complex Whole*. In *The Evolution of Culture*, edited by Robin Dunbar*, et al*, Chris Knight, Robin Dunbar, and Camilla Power examine the cooperative nature of culture; and Ian Watts explores the extension of symbolism beyond reference. Susan Blackmore's *The Meme Machine* argues that humans, mental copy machines, produce group dimensions that influence our cultures and minds as evolution shapes our bodies.

Going beyond narrow projections of techno-supremacy over softer media, John Seely Brown and Paul Duguid examine networks of information within culture in *The Social Life of Information.* Joshua Meyrowitz's *No Sense of Place* considers the implications of culture and location to the expectations of exchange.

At the individual level, both Elaine Morgan in *The Descent of the Child* and Allison Gopnick *et al* in *The Scientist in the Crib* explore the interaction of children with their environment, and learning. Francisco Varela *et al* in *Embodied Knowledge*, and Edward Slingerland in *What Science Offers Humanities*, examine the influence of body and culture on mind.

CHAPTER 11
Visual Thinking and Visual Language

Before proceeding we will explore two manifestations of the influence of vision on mind today. Visual thinking and visual language are important to the future of the mind.

The extension of vision by synthetic augmentation, and the education of vision by post-birth development are increasing the influence of vision on the mind. That influence is most evident today in the thinking and in the language emerging from the collaboration of our neuronal systems and environmental systems—of 'me' and 'not me.'

It is helpful to define terms. I use 'visual' to mean all disturbances registered by sight and evaluated by the self-organizing systems comprising vision. This is distinct from 'graphics' which is more commonly used to describe 'presentations,' electronic or otherwise. Graphics is of the 'not me' perspective. Visual connotes the perspective of 'me,' of my participation with the disturbances that are 'not me.' It is the importance of 'me' in the exchange with 'not me' that is influencing the future of the mind—particularly the language of the visual.

Visual thinking and visual language have become important aspects of culture. Visual thinking focuses on visual perception as a cognitive activity, where thinking—particularly metaphorical thinking—takes place in the realm of imagery. Visual language is an expression of visual metaphors in collaboration with text: STOP, One-way, Do Not Enter—simple, everyday messages better communicated if accompanied by an image.

In our cyber-culture these have become enormously important and are likely to become even more so.

After considering the cyber-culture, we will explore vision as a mode of thinking, and the coming of age of visual language beyond the visually presented sounds of mind. We will examine these two newly aggressive manifestations of the domain of the visual, in the context of visual perception... in the domain of images. In the next chapter we will explore more thoroughly post-birth development in the cyber-culture.

It will be helpful to re-perceive metaphor. As we have seen, metaphor is understanding and experiencing one kind of thing in terms of another. But experience and metaphor are also a function of our bodily interaction with the environment at our boundaries. They are both limited by the modality and structure of those boundaries. Vision emerges from the self-organization of sight with other neuronal systems. Vision is confined by the limits of sight—the boundaries imposed by the physical limitations of sight. The boundaries of vision imposed by sight—our 'field of vision' (pardon the visual metaphor)—both limit and expand the patterns of experience available for use in metaphor. As the 'field of vision' has been augmented by the environmental systems and shared experiences of culture, the boundaries of sight and vision have been extended. The experiences of vision have been expanded, and visual metaphors have become richer in meaning. "He is a bright young man" is obviously based on a different cultural experience than "he was lit up Saturday night!" Or "He is as green as they come" is based on a different experience than "It is a green technology." Visual metaphors such as these are common in our thinking. They will become increasingly so as the synthetic augmentations of culture become more intense.

The Cyber-synthetic Environment

Disturbances under our control are channeling our moves into the adjacent possibilities of visual dominance. Yes. We are creating our own future. Well, perhaps that is too strong. We are influencing the adjacent possibilities that contain our future. How?

Consider. From a chaotic pastiche of light, colors, shapes, and blurred motions, neuronal patterns self-organize in infants. These initial patterns group and overlap, self-organizing into categories for thought and language, establishing life-long biases and initial residual patterns, for perceiving what we see: people, structures, and furnishings... images. These residual patterns comprised of overlapping links and elements throughout the central nervous system, amalgamating the cooperation of all sensuous interfaces, provide a basis for metaphor. We are creating and applying the shaping tools as elements of our culture.

Cultures are extremely influential in the post-birth development of vision. We learn to see in the environment of our culture. Immature senses are stimulated today by the accoutrements and icons of a cyber-augmented culture that inculcates relationships and involvement with computers and computer networks.

The most obvious influence of cyber-augmentation on our pattern recognition and the self-organization of neuronal systems is an intensification of the consequences begun by art, writing, print and the electromagnetic media: the separation of knowledge from knower; abstraction; external storage; remote, private participation in both time and space; and interfaces for mass sharing in real time. It is our cultural mandate to coalesce with these extensions early in life! These visually oriented extensions of self participate in the neuronal self-organizing patterns of self, in the *if-then... or* of visual thinking.

Visual Thinking

We begin with the boundaries and limitations, the opportunities and possibilities of sight. We inherited an extremely complex, versatile system of sight from our arboreal ancestors. Sight is unique among the senses in many ways. The very discrete and partitioned elements of sight originate in dissection yet foment coherence. Sight is fragmented and consolidated, discriminating and coherent, detailed and comprehensive. It is a powerful platform for the emergence of an amorphous, shifting focus of mind provoking abstraction and metaphor. The very fragmentation at first sight is a bonanza for the principal characteristics so useful to metaphor.

Sight, along with hearing and smell, obtains information at a distance. This affords the perceiver the opportunity to be removed from the stimulating phenomenon, to focus on what is happening out there rather than what is happening to me, perhaps providing an opportunity to be more thorough in registration, more deliberate in pattern recognition, and more flexible in response.

Alternative responses depend on the variety of distinctive properties recognizable and organizable into systems of patterns that give leverage to the '*or*' of *if-then... or*. In sight, shapes, colors, movements, and textures are susceptible to complex organizations in space and time—in which they create still another element for organization, depth. The systems of sight are unparalleled in pattern recognition. They are without peer in registering context in complete detail, simultaneously amalgamating the elements into a comprehensive total, while resonating with the transcending, the abstract. Sight is a pillar for the emergence of vision.

We noted in Chapter 6 that vision is selective. The field of vision contends with multiple objects at a time, separating the object of interest from others and context. It actively participates with the environment reaching out for selected objects, registering their surfaces, borders, textures, and colors, simultaneously absorbing their context—in a relentlessly shifting, active interaction.

The active nature of vision integrates the observer and the observed. Sight is the broadband information interface with the environment registering disturbances in almost incomprehensible gulps—registering enormous detail that still confounds some of our best computers. Vision is the super-computer of collaboration and self-organization. The systems and interfaces of vision influence how knowledge and experience is organized and made available, determining the raw material available for the processes of *if-then… or*, and visual metaphor.

Sight provides the opportunity for the body to be disengaged physically, yet the mind can be engaged intensely. The uniqueness of sight is reflected in visual thinking. The vision emerging from these systems is the most powerful component of cognition. In the words of Aristotle, "The soul never thinks without an image." Aristotle was among the first to understand the power of vision in cognition. Visual thinking is *if-then… or* in the modality of vision.

Language is of the sounds of mind. Vision is of the sights of mind. Vision has become increasingly dominant in cognition riding a phase shift begun 50–100,000 years ago—and still underway. Vision is reasserting dominance over the influence of the sounds of mind. The implications of this visual-based thinking are enormous, yet often overlooked in our concentration on the ever expanding self-made tools of electronic environmental disturbance. Perception is about what is happening out there, in the context of what is happening to me. Vision provides a powerful enrichment of the acquisition and evaluation of patterns and the use of metaphor—the coinage of cognition.

Language has long been the province of the sounds of mind and it has embedded the concepts of thinking. That is changing. Visual experiences are also joining in our very thinking. Increasingly, symbols representing sound-embedded concepts are joined with elements representing visual experience to convey enriched meaning.

Visual Language

Visual language is in use today. In visual language, the images of the sights of mind collaborate with the sounds of mind. Visual language combines printed words and visual elements—combining the representations of concepts embedded in both the sounds of mind and the sights of mind. The advertising that blares from all directions is a vivid example of our immersion in visual language.

Images alone may fail to communicate without frequent use, long-term exposure, and universal understanding. Images alone may prevent full participation. They may be exclusive. Yet, the sounds of mind, the words of language, define groups and exclude outsiders from understanding, too. A principal boundary of culture has been language—the sounds of mind. Visual language, incorporating words and images, provides a tether to the sounds of mind, and mitigates the potential ambiguity of visual elements alone. The words of the sounds of mind incorporated with the images of the sights of mind, together, bridge cultures. International traffic signs are an example. An image in a red circle with a red bar going from upper left to bottom right is a clear prohibition.

Words and visual elements together also have the advantage of rapid recognition of the visual element, the abstraction inherent in printed words, better conceptualization, and less ambiguity. There are rules like any language, but they apply to both words and visual elements together.

Historically, our use of synthetic visual environmental elements can be traced back to at least the dawning of cave art, and perhaps further still to the use of icons and markers. In more recent times, starting with the dawning of the computer, we can identify a few points in the evolution of visual language such as flow charts/CPM/PERT diagrams, the introduction of the Graphical User Interface (GUI), visual recording in group meetings, and the visual tsunami of the World Wide Web (WWW). Two of these are of particular interest because they suggest future directions as well as limitations.

The GUI evolved to provide a simple means for directing the computer's actions. By simply 'clicking' on a visual element, an 'icon', the computer could be directed to take a specific action. This interface gave 'me' a simple means for interacting with 'not me,' the computer, and the ever growing network of interactions represented by it. It remains a key interface for directing the computer's actions. The WWW is a protocol, an 'app,' that uses the Internet to link text, images, video, and various multimedia combinations, bringing us a cornucopia of visual elements. But we are getting ahead of ourselves. Let's return to visual language.

Visual language integrates patterns of verbal communications such as words, sentences, and paragraphs, with visual elements in a particular syntax. The study of visual language is a study of how combinations of words and visual elements together communicate meaning. It is how meaning is communicated when words and visual elements are integrated. Horn, in *Visual Language*, explores this phenomenon at length, covering historical development and usage, and provides both semantics and syntax for understanding visual language. As with our spoken language, the rules and regulations governing proper usage are extensive and complex. Yet, as with our spoken language we use visual language effortlessly every day.

The Mind's New Language?

What of visual elements without words? Our exposure to web browsers has taught three generations in many cultures that a funny stick-house is home—a place to start over; green arrows mean back or forward; and an hourglass indicates busy. Will the sounds of mind, the very concepts of thought, continue to monopolize cognition? Will sounds and images of sounds continue to be required? Will the concepts captured in the sounds of mind constrain the free flow of images to a partnership with words? Will the thinking of the soul continue relying on words in the new mind's eye? Perhaps not. Perhaps the sights of mind, the images of experience, will prevail?

We already see evidence of the adjacent possibilities to visual language. The mind's powerful use of metaphor is increasingly dependent on vision. Today we learn the language and categories of images themselves and the concepts embedded in them. From birth, icons introduce us to the shared references of culture. Symbols integrate us into the contextual dimension of group living. Both provoke abstract representations—pattern recognition of the synthetic. In some cultures, toddlers respond to the sight of the Golden Arches, the images on a cereal box, or the neon ice cream cone. In others, the totem of a bear or a hawk; or toys, abstract fish, animals, and airplanes. Children's toy building blocks present cubes, pyramids, arches, and cylinders. Electronic arts entice the mind to interact, to participate, extend, and encompass.

Vision first captured the words and the concepts of sounds through print. Now the use of visual elements alone is expanding in visually oriented professions where jargon already dominates. One of the most celebrated is in one of the most abstract, abstruse fields known to man. Richard Feynman, Nobel laureate in physics, introduced doodles as a means for better understanding quantum physics! In a more mainstream environment, architects use pure icon notation. As electronic augmentation invades their design world, a proposal has been made to use electronic icons, with dimensions of shape, size, height, width, depth, spin direction, spin rate, inside/outside orientation, and movement in space, to convey all the information needed!

Perhaps the use of the Geographic Information System (GIS) demonstrates our current state of transition. GISs are the augmented use of visual metaphor. They were introduced in the 1980s. In a GIS, topology-like visualizations are used to understand relationships of everything from natural resource availability, supply/demand relationships, to technology deployment/cost analyses, to dynamic battlefield tactics. Curiously, a small portion of the population is unable to 'see' the information content of GIS displays! They are unable to understand something else—say supply/demand relationships—in the context of this other experience, a topology map! The topology map is itself a visual metaphor of our experience with the contours of physical land. Nevertheless, for many of us, variations of this technology help us find the nearest coffee house or Indian restaurant, and show us the shortest route between two points.

The World of Visualization

The external, visually oriented environment has emerged with a Lamarckian-like life and culture of its own. We and our augmentations are the basic elements of this CAS with its own initial conditions and adjacent possibilities. While our own contributions may be in part under the happenstance of genes, the augmentations bring initial conditions and adjacent possibilities of their own.

We are surrounded by a self-created, visually seductive environment that molds us from birth. A favored adjunct to our work and understanding is the visualization, the imaging of both everyday and complex analyses of all kinds. We create visualizations to remind us and guide us—participating in our everyday lives. We use dynamic visualizations in three dimensions to represent information of all sorts; and 'tools' to manipulate that visual information ranging from GUI, through retinal projection, to eye-tracking mechanisms. We employ synthetic 'agent-sensors,' cameras and detectors for registering 'visual' information for us in our absence or beyond our physical capacities. All of these tools, designed by us for us, continue the inflation of synthetic visual augmentation begun eons ago.

Visual adjuncts like those listed above are reducing the dimensions of distance and time to marginal considerations. We carry devices in our pockets that extend both our images and the images of our surroundings thousands of miles. We download to 'see' our friends and their activities of yesterday when we awake today. We participate in multiple visual communities with people in remote locations. It is as easy for me to see a friend in Kenya as it is to see my neighbor down the street or a friend's selection while shopping across town. We use these devices to eliminate the limitations of sight imposed by nature—with widespread use of 'false imaging' techniques, shifting nature's light spectrum for our convenience. Facile systems are intensifying our immersion in the visual experience of the synthetic environment.

Self-fulfilling post-birth development, with its increasing emphasis on visualization, creates its own accelerating moves into adjacent possibilities: we are shaped for visualization even as we consume it. From birth our culture prepares us to participate in this augmented visualization while placing a premium on expertise and innovation. We are molded by the augmentation to design the very cyberous augmentations used in our culture to prepare us to design even more cyberous augmentations! The human complex adaptive system is manipulating cyber-synthetic tools, accelerating self-organization into adjacent possibilities dominated by vision.

We are collaborating in an ever-tightening feedback loop. Our own sensuous interfaces are becoming ever more 'tuned-in' to electronic visual disturbances: post-birth development both familiarizes and customizes us from infancy to interact with the synthetic visual augmentations; ever more information essential to daily life is acquired through visualization; we are designing ever more sophisticated visual interfaces; and we are shaping those interfaces for more facile use with our own visual interfaces.

Big Bang in Progress?

In the time scale of evolution, the capabilities of vision are exploding. The systems of sight bequeathed to us by our arboreal ancestors came through eons of self-organizing, slipping, and sliding through adjacent possibilities. In themselves these systems are changing little. But each generation observes the unprecedented pace of change they experience. We are no different. Yet, the pace of change we are experiencing seems truly exponential. The synthetic augmentations we bring to our own visual systems are changing the game. No longer does the slow-time of physical evolution set the pace.

The phase shift that began some 50,000 years ago is relentlessly accelerating, building on the visual achievements of our ancestors with newly derived externalities. The neuronal systems underlying the emergence of our vision provide an almost fantastical color, motion-detection, and registration capability. Our hominid ancestors began augmenting these systems with external aids for representing the environment itself, storing these representations outside of the brain, and retrieving them at will. The cave paintings of tens of thousands of years ago were but the beginning. Today, we have designed augmentations that transform representations of our environment, abstracting them, and substituting for them, in ways that are reminiscent of the brain itself! The electronic picture frame is a simple yet telling example. Where is that photograph in the electronic frame? In memory. In memory? Yes, but in patterns of electrons instead of neurons. It is recallable with more fidelity and more consistency than we ourselves can muster, and it is easily changeable to many other photos that our own memory may not retain. That simple frame augments the brain in the emergence of the mind.

In the long history of the study of mind, mind has been viewed as belonging to an individual. Viewing mind as an emergent property of CASs opens up adjacent possibilities for mind that depart from the hegemony of mind as constrained to the central nervous system of 'me.' The elements of this CAS are not limited to any modality of the senses, to me, or even to reality! Elements in a CAS may even be artifacts *represented* by the execution of software code, of extra-dimensional cyber activity. Consider the artifacts of our culture we have mentioned here. How many of them are simply representations executed by software, electronic bits in silicon?

A mind emerging from systems employing these elements as well as neuronal ones would have a much different capacity than a mind constrained to 'me.' Since emergence occurs from whatever resources are available—including our collective, interacting minds—there is nothing in our understanding of CASs that confines emergence to isolated uniform elements; nor mind to neurons.

The momentum of pattern recognition, self-organizing through eons of adjacent possibilities, is formidable. The collaborating CASs of vision are leaping the boundaries of the nervous system with cyberous augmentation. As the sources of vision multiply, as the underlying systems are augmented still further by our electronic manipulations, where do the limits of cognition lie? The ensuing big bang of metaphor will thrust cognition beyond self. In the next chapter we will explore the nature of the cyberous manifestations in culture—the cradle of post-birth development.

Suggested Additional Reading for Chapter 11

David Abram's *The Spell of the Sensuous* explores earlier visual relationships to natural environments. Rudolf Arnheim's *Visual Thinking* takes us several steps further, exploring the influence of images on cognition. Terrance Deacon, in *The Symbolic Species,* opens our minds to the power of vision, investigating the evolution, structure, and importance of symbols to the mind. Temple Grandin, an autistic, provides a unique perspective on the mind's use of vision in *Thinking in Pictures: and Other Reports from My life with Autism,* describing how her visual memories of circumstances—real, imagined, and abstract—are literally replayed and used to analyze new situations.

Robert Horn's *Visual Language* defines the elements, syntax, semantics, and uses of a new language in use today, flowing out of visual augmentation.

Adam Greenfield, in *Everyware: the Dawning Age of Ubiquitous Computing,* explores the pervasive stretch of cyberous visual augmentation today. Steven Johnson's *Interface Culture* explores our synergistic relationships with rapidly changing electronic environments dominated by images.

CHAPTER 12

Post-Birth Development and Cyberous Culture

Earlier, you were pictured as walking down the street seemingly oblivious to the many disturbances inflicted on your sensuous interfaces: the visual blare of blinking, winking neon and LCDs, the cacophony of vehicles, the monologues of pedestrians talking with unseen companions... and your own absorption with some electronic interface. Closer examination reveals an intriguing symbiosis with our environment hitherto not experienced by any other species. The means for extending our senses into the environment is under the design and direction of the systems being extended—our own systems. These systems are both synthetic and cyber-based. Before exploring the future of the mind it will be helpful to examine the ever tightening relationship between the post-birth development of 'me,' and our culture, the man-made cyberous environment of 'not me.'

Merriam-Webster defines 'synthetic' as "devised, arranged or fabricated for special situations *to imitate or replace usual realities"* [emphasis added]. These cyberous systems are designed, fabricated, and used by ourselves—*to imitate or replace our usual realities—the natural world in which our ancestors lived*. We are designing new realities for ourselves. That's not new. We have self-organized individually and collectively many times. The residual patterns of our nervous systems are self-organizing continuously as we experience life. As members of our cultures we are the participating basic elements of self-organization. Even our imaginations are subject to continuing stimulation and self-organization. This is different. We are designing new realities for ourselves in systems completely external to ourselves! We are designing the future adjacent possibilities for 'me'—out there... in 'not me!'

Merriam-Webster defines 'cyber' as "involving computers or computer networks." Our sensuous systems are being extended beyond the boundaries of our bodies by cyber augmentation—cyberous systems. We contain within the residual patterns of ourselves subtle, yet profound adjacent possibilities. The most obvious influence of cyber augmentation is the intensification of electromagnetic technologies participating in our own pattern recognition.

There is more to cyber augmentations than intensification of previous interactions with our environment. It is more than the intensity of new devices clamoring for our time and attention. We and our cyber augmentation are collaborators in a new kind of symbiotic evolution, one where the instruments of our evolution are being designed by ourselves. We have begun a drift through adjacent possibilities. Not only do we share these possibilities with our cyberous augmentation, but we also collaborate with our cyberous augmentation in those adjacent possibilities—the adjacent possibilities require both of us. The adjacent possibilities of cyberous culture are the adjacent possibilities of ourselves. There are dimensions of cyber augmentation we have ignored.

Out of Sight, Out of Mind

The connectivity and interaction of the complex system of sight, the insatiable reach of the collaborative systems giving rise to the emergence of vision, this whole agglomeration of superior neuronal resources is teaming with the vast resources of the cyber-synthetic environment to give rise to a new emergence out of sight... and out of mind.

Cyber augmentation, seemingly so real, is fantastically abstract and complex beneath the breathtaking visualizations it offers. The environment, now synthetic and self-created, is reaching into the self as never before. A report in the July 15, 2011 issue of *Science* suggests that individuals looking up information in text sources remember the information, while individuals finding the information online remember how to find it... if they need it. We are self-organizing together and with our cyberous culture with an intimacy previously not known. We need only consider the startlingly frank and intimate 'sharing' on Facebook. It is seductively easy to share personal details of our lives with hundreds if not thousands of people. It is just as easy to enter into the personal details of the lives of hundreds of people. The media is filled with anecdotes of surprise and shock when an entry 'goes viral' and haunts the source. Actually, to a young and growing segment of the population it is not startling at all. It is perfectly natural. We spoke earlier of life as just another 'window.' To many, Facebook *is* life. We are no longer intimate with just family and a few friends, but with crowds! Twitter *is* social intercourse. Timely updates are more important than anything physical. We are fomenting an emergence of self and of mind incorporating the elements of the cyberous environment—social media, twitter, blogs, all engage and participate in 'me' with an intimacy of environment as never before.

It bears repeating here that the visual persuasions and seductions of these synthetic cyberous systems are designed *by us* to appeal *to us*, to our visual systems. It begins early. Before we move, we see! Before we learn to walk, to talk, we learn to see. Our eyes move, register, and self-organize patterns from birth. Hierarchies of sight-stimulated residual patterns collaborate and self-organize while we lie flat on our backs, gurgling with our thumbs in our mouths. Cyberous systems pump up this self-organization, joining in this mélange of sights—of colors, shapes, and textures moving in front of sight's registration.

Self-organization is also a feature of the systems constituting the cyberous environment—our cyberous culture. The characteristics of technological evolution evidence all of the aspects of CASs: initial conditions, adjacent possibilities, collaborative combinations, and the importance of sequences—characterized as lock-in, hierarchies, and emergence—within the agency of *Homo sapiens*. Cyberous systems do evolve. Literally. Our smartphone lies patiently waiting for us to wake in the morning. It sits there with the initial condition we left it in last night—including the alarm that reaches out to us at the proper time, or it may download information for us as we sleep. The entire network at its disposal has been collaborating, slipping through adjacent possibilities as we sleep. A whole sequence of interactions has taken place stimulated by those who are not sleeping, and by electronically provoked adjustments, updates, and new capabilities we have yet to meet. These actions are not initiated by 'me,' but they await me when I awake. They have taken place without me in the cyberous culture that is both 'not me' and a serious collaborator in what I am… of 'me.' These changes occur in the environment with respect to me—not in me.

The elements of cyberous culture participate in the self-organization of post-birth development, rapidly multiplying throughout culture, increasingly facile and supple in character, blurring boundaries between self and environment, and between real and unreal. What exactly are social networks? Disturbances we initiate ripple through this cyber fabric on a scale approaching that of the brain. The phenomenal reach, focus, and grasp of simply 'Googling' are beyond comprehension. We encounter the cyber persona of others even as our own is extended with online personalities through blogs, social networks, and avatars. Yet, only one early cyberous web-based game, Majestic, has actually admitted to playing us! How many others are there?

Feedback between these cyberous systems and our own is designed by us to be inherent in us, virtually from birth, with intuitive interfaces fashioned for transparent exchange. Cyberous systems have opened adjacent possibilities most useful to vision. It is the intense visualization delivered by these systems, the access to our systems of vision, the fodder for visual metaphor that distinguishes them from the natural targets of our senses—accelerating a journey through adjacent possibilities that has been eons in duration.

We continue the phase shift begun 50,000 years ago. Prosthetic augmentation is unnecessary, though a popular notion in the media. Nor are we simply using new tools. We have created a new environment into which we have extended ourselves as participants and introduced ourselves as tools. The sensuous and the cyberous are coalescing. We are wired!

Today's Legacy

No new physical developments are required of our nervous system for this future of the mind. We need not wait for evolution, for self-organizations through adjacent possibilities to prepare us. Our neural systems are equipped, quivering at the start for the next move along the edge of chaos. The legacies of our eons-long journey through adjacent possibilities of pattern recognition, vision, and post-birth development—each is primed and prepared to move into cyberous opportunities. So too are the cyber-synthetic environmental systems of our own making. There is a long history of the evolution of technology presently culminating in the phase shift into cyberous systems.

There are, of course, the purely physical augmentations. The computer mouse and its variations are means for representing ourselves in cyberspace; the desktop is prototypical of structures for self-organization; and portability provides for constant, relentless, interaction: GPS chips, personal identification tags, and soon-to-be implants are means for our cyberous culture to keep in touch with us, and us with it. These put us in the game. There will be more physical augmentations. But this is not the place to chronicle the obvious. The seduction of our legacies is deeper and more profound.

Video games best illustrate the potential of cyber augmentation. It is widely believed that video game players develop attention deficit, disengage from real life, and experience poor academic performance. But research into people using role-playing, fantasy video games demonstrates just the opposite. Students proficient in these video games are better scholars than those who are not, and better decision-makers in real life. There is a direct relationship between the extent of video game proficiency and academic achievement. A strenuous workout with video games leads to increased mental muscularity. How?

Research indicates that video games take sensuous augmentation into new territory in three ways.

Most striking is the variability they introduce, the choices they force, and the consequences of those choices to the participant. Print, movies, and TV are linear, passive. There is one beginning, one end, and one path between. The creator decides on the beginning, the plot, and the end. We are passive consumers. Whereas video games have multiple endings and numerous ways of achieving them. Participants make decisions, choose strategies and tactics. They take action. The consequences and rewards of their decisions vary. Cumulative decisions lead to different endings. No one series of actions, no single set of decisions, is correct.

Video games also force participants to accept responsibility. They reward success. They allow participants to use rewards as *they* wish to improve *their* chances for future success. The manner and timing of rewards encourage participants to explore, to test, to learn.

Most profoundly, video games respond to our learning. They adapt with us. They participate with us. They self-organize with us. These systems monitor our successes, become increasingly difficult as our skills increase, induce us to reach ever more into the cyber environment and reward us for doing so successfully. In video game lingo, this maintains us in the 'regime of competency' in which a player's participation is incubated within a set of rules, challenges, and rewards designed to encourage participation, even while the skills of the player are extended by the game. As the player's skills improve, the game increases the skills required in a spiral of ever increasing challenge, reward, and expertise. Games keep us on the cutting edge of our performance. This is eerily similar to a CAS moving into adjacent possibilities as fast as possible while maintaining the integrity of the system—skirting the edge of chaos. The brain's use of dopamine is related to learning. Video games increase the flow of dopamine. Video games incorporate sound principles of learning.

Culture is the original regime of competency—a group's set of rules and relationships, challenges and rewards are initially within reach of most. Today, the elements of culture, themselves self-organizing in response to stimulation, present ever developing opportunities and challenges, ever more augmenting interfaces, and a seemingly endless number of cyberous systems for collaboration with neuronal ones for those with the skills to respond.

Our moves through this sequence of cyberous adjacent possibilities, each with its initial conditions, each with its rules, competencies and rewards, each enticing more extensive and elaborate collaboration with that which is 'not me,' has been subtle, perhaps even seductive. In the light of the initial attractiveness of post-birth development, e.g. support of survival, post-birth development among humans has now far surpassed that initial attractiveness. It has far surpassed any threshold required for simply surviving. Post-birth development, the essence of our environment, has achieved a momentum of its own in tight interaction and feedback with our sensuous interfaces. John Wooden once said that "once we are finished learning, we are finished." A true gamer.

What does this process of learning, this intense, incessant process of residual pattern reorganization in collaboration with the cyberous environment, mean to the future of the mind?

Cyberous systems impose focus and context. Their rules are filters, facilitating interaction with information. Yet they constrain what information can itself be, how we perceive information, and how we relate to it. Visual metaphors like the 'desktop' direct not only our visual attention but also our perception, and conceptualization of information.

Infants are fine-tuned from birth to self-organize in collaboration with systems we create, systems to which we expose them. Today, the infant's visual bootstrap-self-organizing takes place in a cyberous environment. Toddlers interact with increasingly seductive cyberous interfaces at early ages. Children learn that cyberous systems are responsive to them: residual patterns they create remain with the cyberous systems.

The Power of the Adjacent

We need only follow the most fundamental of evolution and complexity theory. Follow the ruts that work into the adjacent possibilities: the path of least resistance.

There is nothing mysterious about adjacent possibilities or the propensity to explore them. This is not science fiction. Where we stand determines where we may take our next step. How we are prepared enables our next act. What we know determines what we may learn. Residual patterns channel the possibilities of the next self-organization. As all CASs do, cyberous cultures present initial conditions and adjacent possibilities for exploration—for gamers and for the cyberous cultures themselves. A cyberous culture is one emerging from those elements which include cyberous elements. New networks, new interfaces, new sites, new operating systems, new possibilities of all kinds are tried, succeed or fail. The World Wide Web (WWW) was an adjacent possibility of the initial conditions of the Internet. Web browsers such as Safari, Firefox, and Internet Explorer were adjacent possibilities to the WWW. Now Apps—applications—are another adjacent possibility of the Internet, operating independently of the WWW and browsers. Smartphones were an adjacent possibility of cellphones, mainframe computers to minis to desktop Personal Computers to laptops to notebooks to tablets to... on and on! All depended on initial conditions and the sequence of adjacent possibilities—both cyberous and human acceptance. All had false starts along the way—adjacent possibilities not taken.

Already, the enhanced performance of gamers is not confined to games. Research indicates gaming improves pattern recognition, systems thinking, patience and delayed gratification, and prioritization. Gamers dramatically improve speed and scope of *visual perception* compared to non-gamers. Practice with games decreases the mental effort required for a task. Gamers who are professionals—doctors, lawyers, managers—make fewer errors, are more sociable, more confident, and more comfortable solving problems creatively. Cyberous culture is already making a dramatic difference in the residual patterns of self and in the adjacent possibilities of life... right before our eyes.

What adjacent possibilities are not so obvious? Which ones are we less capable of seeing, of researching, of anticipating? The rules and the consequences of playing, of interacting with the cyberous transcend the mental workout of video games. The rules and interactions of culture, of our relationships with one another, are in flux even as we increase our interactions with the synthetic. Consider the implications for adjacent possibilities.

We now have lives in the synthetic world where the rules of exchange, the relationships, and collaborations are less about self than about interaction and collaboration. Many consider their Facebook page or hashtag more a part of their 'self' than their physical systems. The self is incidental to the exchange, an element in the system. The cyberous environment offers opportunities for virtual lives of incredible diversity—whole worlds of avatars, cyberous social relationships, from the dull and mundane to the exotic, bizarre and even those that transgress the rules of our physical culture.

These are relationships and collaborations without location, without the references of physical environment—without the environment of nature, cultural relationships and rules, and palpable self-organization. The rules of collaboration and interaction we associate with where we are, the physical surroundings and grounding of our cultural environment, are not operative in these cyberous places. The 'selfs' in cyberous culture reach out through sensuous extensions from wherever they are, from whatever location-culture they inhabit—or want to escape. In cyberous culture there is no place! There is no there, there! What happens to post-birth development when there is no place, no 'there' for reference, for home-base? What happens to the future of the mind?

These lives in the synthetic world are apart from the registrations, the self-organizations, and the residual patterns within the boundaries of 'me.' These extensions of self—these pattern registrations, self-organizations, and pattern recognitions are part of 'not me,' yet they collaborate transparently with the boundary that is 'me.' Where has 'I' gone? Where is 'I' going?

Shakespeare said "All the world's a stage and all the men and women merely players." It is as if we have unconsciously become elements on some larger stage, a swarm of mind elements... merely players.

Metaphor... To the Power!

The power of the visual interface with the external environment will enable a transcendent level of metaphorical cognition beyond anything we can imagine. Will we be the Homo Archaic of the future? Will the *Homo* line of the future look back at us as we look back at archaic *Homo sapiens*—not quite there? Are we part of the future, or the past in this dawning cyberous culture? Metaphor is traceable to our most fundamental roots: to that time of our first understanding of the other. Metaphor has brought us to where we are. Metaphor of the cyberous culture will include our experience with the cyberous. It will be of experience using the modalities and the interactions at our extended synthetic boundaries. There will be an increase in the scope and basis available for metaphor as we move into the adjacent possibilities of this augmented post-birth development. There will be more sources, more patterns for understanding one thing in terms of another. These patterns will be cyberous and they will be collaborating with 'me' in the future of the mind.

Infants begin registration, self-organization, and recognition of neural patterns by first using broad categories of elements such as dog, or fish, and then progressing into more complex patterns and recognition of sub-categories such as bulldog and spaniel, or porpoise and shark. Limited experience is used to maximum advantage. As experience is gained, and registrations increase, as the number of residual patterns having overlapping and related elements accumulate, simple rules self-organize into sub-categories and relationships emerge. These initial and continuing registrations have now been joined by our cyberous culture in the cocoon of post-birth development.

Residual patterns self-organizing within cyber systems are intensifying—outside self, into all of those adjacent possibilities behind the simple display of your smartphone or your tablet. The stimulations of these patterns—passwords, messages, bookmarks, blogs, records, entries, searches, personal organization of information—as with the systems themselves, are products of our 'selfs.' Still others are of the systems themselves. Under the visual metaphors shaping information and knowledge are preferences, routing priorities, cookies, pies, links, spam and anti-spam and fire walls, system permissions, agents, viruses—all self-organizing within these systems, seemingly at our behest.

Finally, the residual patterns of self are increasingly under the sway of the systems we create. Print changed the process of thinking. What will cyberous systems do to our thinking, to our selfs? The cyberous experiences will be more interactive and more intense than our natural, physical ones, registering more sensuous-extended, synthetic disturbances, accumulating residual patterns both within and without the 'self' as we know it—enabling higher level 'modeling,' enabling more categories for interacting, in turn leading to more complex metaphorical thinking. The consequences will be of experiences we have not yet had. The metaphors will be of things we do not yet know.

Will this cyberous-cultural, post-birth development, self-organize residual patterns of new cognitive levels that will differentiate our descendants from us? Likely, but we do not know. We are only elements in this cyberous culture, this CAS.

The New Mind's Eye

What will the new mind's eye see? What will it think? Complexity theory holds that there is no way of knowing the property that will emerge from a self-reorganizing CAS—one succeeding us, or encompassing us. But there are suggestions in the trajectories we ride today.

In oral cultures, mythic descriptions of events are an important means for bringing the lessons of the past to bear on the present, but these same events, reduced to writing, became fixed as specific events unalterable for shaping or fitting the circumstances of the present. Initial visual media continued this scheme. But over the last 40,000 years there has been a dizzying acceleration into adjacent possibilities as the interaction of the nervous system and the environment was drawn ever more to the interface of sight and the emergence of vision—to a broadband interface interacting with environmental disturbances designed and controlled by the self. Today, events of past, present, and future, of imagination and fact, can be indistinguishable. They can be freely manipulated to influence the present, the future, or our memories of the past.

A series of articles in the July 2013 issue of the IEEE's publication, *Computer*, is suggestive of a new direction of collaboration with the cyberous. The new field of Visual Analytics, combining computer graphical presentation of 'big data', and human visual pattern recognition and reasoning, has the promise of solving problems *we do not fully understand and are unable to specify ... or problems of which we are not aware*! That seems a little unsettling!

What of the cyberous systems themselves? What will they see? During a threat to public safety in New York in 2010, the records of over 80 privately operated security video cameras in the space of a few city blocks were available for analysis together with an undisclosed number of police videos. Eerily comparable to the eye of the fly! There are almost daily reports of events captured by cellphone videos—from the personal to the institutional, 'seeing' anything from personal events to masses in action. Face recognition software is being deployed. Inevitably, the adjacent possibilities of new algorithms will bring this all together for our cyberous augmentation to share in a new mind's eye.

Before proceeding to the future of the mind, let us pause for a coda. Each CAS gives rise to an emergent property from the connections and interactions of its elements. That property exceeds the sum of the parts of the CAS; cannot be predicted by examination of the elements, nor of the connections and interactions; and is qualitatively different than the elements of the CAS.

We evolve. Cyberous systems evolve. The cyberous systems comprising the WWW qualify as a CAS. The adjacent possibilities are unknown to us. The next technology waiting in the next niche, the next adjacent possibility, is beyond our sight. There will be new interactions of cyberous systems with our neural systems, new emergent properties.

What of *Homo sapiens*? Post-birth development in a cyberous culture marks a transition from the physical evolution of the past. We have explored this past with a confidence supported by fossils. The little known realm of mental change—of moves into adjacent possibilities of mental reorganization—is more difficult to trace. Changes in the mind, scarcely known from historical physical evidence, are now the tendency into adjacent possibilities. Instead of the physical change of the past, *Homo sapiens* marks a new line that is still emerging—a line manifesting change in emergent mind! Is it *Homo cyber*? Or is it cyberous homo? Or...?

What will happen to our residual neuronal patterns? What will happen to the self? What will be The Future of the Mind? It is time to explore that future.

Suggested Additional Reading for Chapter 12

Brian Arthur's *The Nature of Technology: What it is and How it Evolves* presents a theory of the evolution of technology itself—evolution that is eerily influenced by initial conditions and adjacent possibilities, seemingly undergoes stasis and phase shifts, and increases exponentially.

Donald Michael in *Technology and the Management of Change*, an essay in *In Search of the Missing Elephant*, explores the interaction of technology and culture. Jaron Lanier's *You Are Not a Gadget* illustrates the importance of initial conditions and adjacent possibilities in the evolution and organization of technology, humanity, and their interaction. Sherry Turkle's *Life on the Screen* explores how our relationships within the cyberous culture are changing our minds and testing the validity of self. Joshua Meyrowitz's *No Sense of Place* explores the consequences of cyberous interaction in the absence of common cultural foundations.

James Paul Gee's *What Video Games Have to Teach Us About Learning and Literacy*, explores the learning dimensions of video games that incorporate role-playing and fantasy characters, the principles of learning, and the consequences to gamers of playing. Marc Prensky's *Don't Bother Me Mom—I'm Learning* examines the first generation to grow up entirely in the digital games milieu (under thirties), their relationships with digital games, and the sub-systems and systems in which both the games and the gamers interact—perhaps a game-changing phase shift in itself. John Beck and Mitchell Wade, in *Got Game; How the Gamer Generation is Reshaping Business Forever*, evaluate the gamer generation in business and the professions. The July 2013 issue of IEEE's publication, *Computer*, provides a review of the current state of Visual Analytics, in which the strengths of computer graphical visualization of 'big data' are used in collaboration with human pattern recognition.

Ray Kurzweil's *The Singularity is Near* provides a perspective on the coalescing of technology and humanity in an ever tightening circle. Two books provide perspectives from opposite sides of the cyberous-culture/mind interface. Adam Greenfield, in *Everyware: the Dawning Age of Ubiquitous Computing*, explores contemporary cyberous systems influencing and participating in the evolution of the mind. Gary Small and Gigi Vorgan, in *iBrain: Surviving the Technological Alteration of the Modern Mind*, review generational differences in adaptation to the cyberous culture.

PART FOUR

The Future of the Mind: a Re-Perception

We will explore three futures of the mind. In Chapter 13 we will discuss a mind that is increasingly more unknowable than the current model. The trajectory of vision, augmented by, and collaborating with, our cyberous culture, will dominate this future. In Chapter 14 we will consider a mind that is an absentee mind—literally out of our body. Pattern recognition will dominate this future. In Chapter 15 we will consider our mind as one contributing to, or more accurately subsumed by, an emerging mind that transcends our individual minds. Ironically, post-birth development will enable both our collaboration in this mind and our being subsumed by it. We will explore these three futures individually, but they will likely coincide in our future. In this book, I have suggested re-perceptions of several terms. For convenience they are repeated in the boxes of this introduction to Part Four, as we begin exploring the future of the mind.

The trajectories we have traced and are projecting into the future have durations of thousands of millennia, and the phase shift of which we are a part has been underway thousands of years. Considering these time intervals with our life spans of mere tens of years, we should not expect to experience a Hollywood like metamorphosis into some science fiction creature with an enlarged head and bulging eyes. Yet we are experiencing the changes of the phase shift and these changes are suggestive of the future of the mind.

In Chapter 1, I used an example from economic theory—a shift in demand, to illustrate the phase-shift currently underway in the mind. The evidence we have explored suggests that such a redefining event began in the construct of the mind about 50,000 years ago—plus or minus a few thousand years.

> A pattern is a fully realized form, or model acceptable or proposed for imitation.

In the time-scale of evolution, it is reasonable to believe this shift is still under way: visual input is becoming more important to our mind; the importance of synthetic augmentation to our senses, to our selfs, to our minds is still accelerating; the blossoming of visual pattern recognition and metaphor is of increasing importance to our cognition; and our reliance on elements of mind is not simply neural. In Chapter 8 we explored the three phases of increasing intelligence, changes in internal representation, and increasing versatility. Do we see evidence of increasing intelligence moving into a phase four? What is happening to the processes of representation with the increasing participation of cyberous systems? Is the mind more versatile with more augmentation? The cyberous is not simply augmenting... it has become collaborative.

We have focused on the expression of interactions among biological neural systems interacting with the environment. We have considered the progression of augmentation to our senses, to our boundaries, and the acceleration of full collaboration of the cyberous with our experiences and to the very boundaries of self. I believe the adjacent possibilities include futures of the mind in which the boundaries and experiences of the cyberous will be as much ours as are the sensuous experiences we so routinely embody today. Yet, indications are that this transition is only beginning. Why?

The current state of metaphor and the cyberous suggests we are only at the beginning of this phase transition. Metaphor facilitates understanding of one thing in the context of another. Metaphor uses two domains: the domain of origin, the one of prior common or shared experience that provides a basis for understanding something new; and a metaphorical domain of the new thing to be understood. Today, concepts such as social networks, or cloud computing, are rarely used to facilitate understanding of

> Metaphor is understanding or experiencing one kind of thing in terms of another. Here, the term is further used to describe those instances when characteristics of pre-existing residual neural patterns are enlisted to promote the registration, assimilation, and understanding of a newly encountered environmental pattern.

something new. They are appearing in metaphors in the second domain— the thing needing understanding and explanation. Our experiences with other events or processes are used to assist our understanding of these relatively new cyberous concepts. We are not yet commonly using cyberous concepts to increase our understanding of other new concepts we encounter. There are beginnings.

Over the last 30–40 years our experience with computers *has* led to such metaphors as "When she retired she re-programmed her life" or "I'm having trouble up-loading that" (memory lapse), or "I must have misplaced that disk" (again, memory lapse). Yet, despite the media buzz, our collaboration with the broader cyberous world is still progressing through early adjacent possibilities. We have not yet completely embodied these systems and their boundaries, and our experiences with those boundaries, *as our own*. Nor, we might consider, have they fully embodied us—a phenomenon we should anticipate in the context of CASs. That may be the dividing line between ourselves and our more cyberous descendants. There are some hints of what is to come. It was quick as a tweet! Or simply, I friended her! Does that mean the same thing as she is my friend? Probably not. These are crude examples, and significantly perhaps, our children could do better. But the path is open. Until we have sufficient experiences with the *cyberous* boundaries of 'me,' until there is a shared base of cyberous experiences for use in metaphor, there will not be such metaphor.

Essential to the increased sophistication of the acquisition and use of patterns, has been the emergence of an integrated registration of patterns—a realm of subjectivity we identify as self. Meaning is *to* a cohesive system, *to* 'me.' Something must be meaningful *to*

> 'Self' is *the residual state, at any given time*, of a continuously self-organizing human nervous system interacting with the environment to which it is exposed.

me, or *to* you. If there is no registration at the boundary of a cohesive system, there is no disturbance to that system, no meaning to the system. This subjectiveness is a basic, if not primitive, aspect of the self. The human mind is traditionally defined as subjective in that it includes elements of the self. We have not traditionally defined mind as including elements external to the self—a subjective realm in which elements of the environment are included. This subjective realm is a formidable obstacle to our understanding of the future of the mind. We must address it in any discussion of the future of the mind.

Perhaps unexpectedly, we will appreciate the profound implications of post-birth influences, the intrusive nurturing of post-birth development of culture on the self-organizing and functioning of neural systems.

As we evaluate the future of

> Cognition is the coalescence of all the self-organizing patterns of the human nervous system collaborating in receiving, storing, and processing disturbances—the operation of perception, recognition, learning, and response. It is the effecting of *if-then react thus... or react in another manner*, based on the nervous system's experience with environmental disturbances.

the mind, we must also address a paradox. On the one hand, the evolution of our capability for expressing rapid, coded sounds in the formation of language has contributed mightily to our cognitive abilities; has enabled the interaction of numerous systems and sub-systems forming our body's internal mind; has enabled extensive interaction among multiple minds; and has supported the synthetic augmentations of the senses, and thus an enhanced consciousness, self, and mind. The very compression of vast concepts into simple sounds facilitates both an understanding of what is happening to 'me,' to self, and what is happening out there. Imagine consciousness, self, and mind without the sounds of mind.

On the other hand, the most primitive and the most powerful interactions among the components of mind are metaphor-based, and the most powerful metaphor-based interactions employ the patterns self-organized in the extensive systems informing and giving emergence to vision. Visual experiences stimulate verbally, sound based expression of

> Consciousness is a process. It is the *current state of interaction* between the human nervous system and the environment, or *interaction* among the systems comprising the human nervous system, or a combination of the two.

metaphors—we see a rose and speak of rosy cheeks. The broadband of cognition is visual. However, the last mile, the dial-up mode of cognition, is through words and the sounds of mind. Furthermore, neither of the two modes—visual or sound—is independent of the other. In our consideration of the future of the mind, these two modes must resolve into reasonable accommodation. Wherever our minds go from here, it will be into the adjacent possibilities of the visual and the sounds of mind. We shall consider if that holds for minds that are not 'ours.'

Perhaps the most profound issue of all is the role of external systems in the future emergence of mind. For most of the last 50,000 years these systems have simply augmented our own systems. Now they are collaborators in the emergence of mind. Have we appropriately defined mind?

> The mind is that property emerging from the self-organizing of the self, stimulated by the interaction of the self with the environment. This emergent property is driven by consciousness, the process of the interaction.

What might we gain in understanding by stepping back and re-perceiving the mind as having elements that are both organic and non-organic? What might we gain by re-perceiving the mind as emerging from a system having basic elements drawn from both neural systems and external systems? Exploring the future of mind will require such a re-perception.

CHAPTER 13

Our Increasingly Unknowable Mind

You have read the first twelve chapters, or perhaps you jumped to Part Four, or maybe impatiently to this sentence. How did you do that? How did you read? That is unknowable! Antonio Damasio in *Descartes' Error* points out that the processes manipulating representations, what I call patterns, operate sub rosa to mind. We do not know of them. This phenomenon of not knowing is not new. Neither is it a particularly unsettling prospect. It has long been an operating aspect of the human mind. This chapter is about an unrelenting increase in mind that is unknowable. What do we mean by unknowable? What does that mean to 'me?' And how do pattern recognition, vision, and post-birth development lead us there?

We will explore two dimensions of the unknowable. The first, according to Merriam-Webster is, "not knowable; *especially: lying beyond the limits of human experience or understanding*" [emphasis is mine]. Alternatively, what is 'knowable?' Again courtesy of Merriam-Webster, 'knowable' is "to perceive directly: have direct cognition of." These definitions will be useful reference points for us.

The second dimension of the unknowable mind is the one observed by Antonio Damasio. Our exploration will include both. Unknowable is appropriate for aspects of a mind that increasingly emerges from the self-organizing experience of multiple neuronal *and* cyberous systems, from both known *and* alien modalities of disturbance. But the phrase *beyond the limits of human experience* presents an unsatisfactory dilemma. How do we describe something beyond the limits of our experience, beyond the capabilities of our boundary modalities, beyond our senses? The past is not likely to be of much assistance here. We could simply explore the 'unknown' mind—those lapses or omissions of consciousness that we routinely ignore: the processes of walking, or talking, for example—or those ahaa moments, or even those metaphors that crop up mysteriously. These are unknowable. But that is not only where this unknowable mind is going.

Let's build this up slowly. First, we will set the stage, so to speak: how the trajectories of vision, pattern recognition and post-birth development will continue. We will also explore two possible constraints on this future of mind—the sounds of mind and the subjective realm of self; and close with some factors today signaling the emergence of this mind.

Setting the Stage

Our lives are filled with lapses or omissions of mind, or perhaps even a lack of attention, or focus. These instances are *of* human experience and cognition. They are neither unknowable nor knowable in the sense we want to explore here.

There are hints of the unknowable mind in our experiences. Those sudden insights, the ahaas you feel so good about when they occur, these provide an entry point for us. So do metaphors, those transfers of understanding—those shared experiences that allow us to jump from one cognitive experience to the understanding of another, unrelated one. The hierarchies of mind itself, reflected in these works of mind, are unknown to us. Remember, our experience, our perception, is through the modalities of our senses—our interfaces with the 'not-me.' The operations of the vast subterranean mashup of sub-systems in the elements of mind itself, giving emergence to the mind as whole, are not traceable 'causes' of that emergence. The mind does not engage in the collaboration of its elements. It simply emerges from the consequences of that collaboration. The collaboration is unknowable. We cannot 'experience' these collaborations. But all of these are still *of* our experience.

The second source of the unknowable is more profound. It is well to consider that the mind is a consequence, an emergence of self-organization, not an objective. Nor is mind unified. I have included in Chapter 5 examples of mind disabled or dysfunctional in part yet functioning in whole. The mind we know arises from mind's elements self-organizing among themselves to give emergence to mind as a whole. That consequence—mind—increasingly flows from the influence of disturbances and collaborations stemming from cyberous, 'not me' sources. These are leading to truly unknowable aspects of mind we have not previously encountered as a species.

These are the two aspects of unknowable mind we will explore. There are three dimensions of interest: alien modalities, the 'experiences' of cyberous systems, and the post-birth experience of culture.

Alien Modalities

The trajectory of vision dominates this future of mind. It is through vision that alien modalities of patterns are introduced to the mind. Vision registers the translations and interpretations of alien modalities for collaboration with the pattern recognition of natural systems—ours. The multiple modalities of our five senses are integral to the mashup of our collaborating central nervous system and to the elements of mind. We know that our systems interact and self-organize in concert with systems of the cyberous environment. These systems have their own modalities and rules for self-organization, their own residual states, and their own adjacent possibilities. They are alien. They are beyond the limits of human experience, beyond the capacity of our boundaries to register them as disturbances. Yet with the augmentation of devices of our own design, we do register them.

We have designed systems to translate phenomena beyond our perception into our own modalities, into a means for registering the disturbances in alien modalities. We have enlisted the systems of vision to include the unknowable. We 'read' the x-ray image of our bones produced by a machine. When alien modalities registering alien disturbances are translated into disturbances that stimulate our mind, these become part of mind. The interfaces we have designed to facilitate exchange with alien modalities and collaboration with the systems using them are increasing the unknowable dimension of mind. How? What and where are those unknowable disturbances?

What of those false images we encounter in the media? From weather maps to quantum mechanics to cosmology, our understanding has increased immensely in recent decades and the pace of our increase in knowledge is accelerating. These images are not of human experience. We do not sense them. Do we *know* them through our corporeal senses, through the modalities of our own interfaces, of our own registrations? When is the last time a human experienced a black hole or a quark? These are unknowable to us. They are beyond the limits of our experience. The modalities of which they are a part are brought to us in forms we perceive—through interfaces that not only augment our own registrations and self-organizations, but link our cognition to the very cyberous systems augmenting our own. Behind those interfaces are vast numbers of disturbances, registrations, and pattern recognitions that are beyond anything we can experience. *The Black Hole*, a 1979 science fiction movie, struggled to portray what it would be like to fall into a black hole. It was not convincing. It was beyond the limits of our experience. We may have models, simulations that 'explain' and predict black holes or quarks, but they are beyond the limits of human experience. They are unknowable.

There are more everyday examples. We use the detection of magnetic fields to indicate true North, and 'night goggles' for detecting infra-red radiation. Then there are those ubiquitous screens we carry around with us whose systems capture, analyze, and display pulses of radiation as information. Our systems are captives of alien modalities which are beyond the limits of our experience, beyond our cognition, beyond knowing—brought to us by the collaboration of vision.

The systems of these alien modalities have their own hierarchies which, in collaboration, become our own and embodied into our knowing. Just as are the hierarchies operating in the brain. Their disturbances, residual patterns, self-organizations and emergences, in collaboration with ours, become ours. Not so, you say? Consider the state of cosmology, physics, or the accomplishments of engineering; without the assistance of these alien modalities we cannot see, touch, or hear much of the physical world of which we are a part. Imagine the state of medicine without x-rays or MRIs.

At all levels and within all biological and cyberous systems, the rules for self-organizing are moving through adjacent possibilities. The central nervous system will respond to the opportunities and the influences presented by the synthetic environment, and achieve adjacent states with the resources and capabilities available at the time. Physical change offered at any hierarchical level in adjacent possibilities will be tested in the environment and adopted if consistent with the rules of self-organization; but physical change is not necessary.

The cyberous systems themselves are expanding in scope and complexity beyond any real accounting. All of these self-organizing together, with their own diverse modalities, provide a heady broth for the mind's emergence.

The Experience of Cyberous Systems

Beyond their alien modalities, the layers of cyberous systems have the same unknowability within their 'sub rosa' manipulation. These cyberous systems collaborating with our neural ones are unknowable to us. It is in these systems that we find the continuation of the trajectory of pattern recognition.

Consider the information acquisition of a simple Google search on the Web. The Web itself has rules for interaction—addresses, formats and parsing, levels of organization and operation, hierarchies of instructions, interfaces, feedback, internal languages—each element contributing to the Web's continuous self-organization. Here, too, sequences and initial conditions matter. The multitude of systems requesting access, providing data in various modalities, analysis, information acquisition, and presentation gives rise to a chaotic world of which we can sense nothing, to patterns that are unknowable to us. This is a world of residual patterns, stimulation, self-organization and emergent properties unknowable to us… yet a world collaborating in the emergence of our mind.

These systems register change in their environments. They experience change. Experience? Their residual patterns are disturbed and self-organize into adjacent possibilities with new residual patterns. They change with the circumstances stimulating them. They recognize patterns and they self-organize patterns of residuals in response to disturbances of the environment. Their residual patterns reflect a history of disturbances, of change. They learn.

Consider the Google 'crawler.' It is designed to keep up with the experience of cyberous systems. It is designed to track the experience— the changes in the residual patterns—of these cyberous systems. This software, characterized as a crawler because of its mode of operation, continuously travels throughout the vastness of the Web noting the to-us-insensible changing cyberspace patterns of information available. The crawler registers these observations within the Google system, which in turn 'recognizes' it for us on request, seamlessly connecting us to the information and translating whatever modality it may have originated in or been stored in. What incredible machinations are going on behind our captivating display screens! These systems have their own yet-to-be-appreciated patterns ebbing and flowing within them, as well as the capacity for recognizing those patterns, and resonating and responding to them. And, yet, to us it is literally child's play all brought to us on our smartphone… and contributing to the emergence of our mind.

What of the patterns observed by the crawler and preserved for our collaboration? What of the patterns translated and parsed for recognition and resonance in the domains of our sensuous interfaces; patterns of experience we have not had *and could not have*; patterns preserved for participation in our self-organization, in our mind? The translations are of familiar domains—images and sounds—and they are of alien domains—images of the un-seeable, sounds of the un-hearable, and analyses of the unimaginable and unknowable. These patterns collaborate in the emergence of *our* minds. *Our* minds emerge from disturbances, registrations, the self-organization of residual patterns, and pattern recognitions which are unknowable to us. Where does the Bay Bridge begin? Where is 'me?'

The trajectory of pattern recognition we explored in natural systems continues, but it is now augmented by and collaborating with synthetic systems of our own design. The implications and consequences will show up in metaphor and cognition.

The processes of metaphor are not known to us. Yet, metaphor is so integrated with the experience of the senses that it is virtually a sense in its own right. Aristotle observed that "Ordinary words convey only what we already know; it is from metaphor that we can best get hold of something fresh." Metaphor supports cognition, experience sponsors metaphor, patterns register experience, and the senses mediate the patterns of experience with the environment. With cyberous augmentation of the patterns of experience, metaphor and cognition will have an expanded base. The patterns flowing from our senses will be joined by the patterns of alien modalities appropriately translated to our own. Those experiences we have through cyberous collaboration and translation will coalesce with those we experience in the window of life. The consequence will be an expansion and enrichment of the patterns for metaphor—and cognition.

Are there hints of what is to come? They are rare. Heard among young mothers at a mall in Silicon Valley, "the three-year-old's mind is like a crawler!" (Searching relentlessly?) Or at the office, "his desk is a black hole." (What goes in never comes out?) Curious. Both crawlers and black holes are beyond the limits of human experience, yet used in metaphors they provide understanding of other things in their terms—which are unknowable!

The Post-Birth Experience of Cyberous Culture

We have distinguished post-birth development as of 'me,' from the influence of cultures as 'not me.' Culture, as the dominant 'not me,' is increasing the unknowable as it channels post-birth development into the adjacent possibilities of the cyberous. Synthetic augmentation will increasingly dominate post-birth development and the emergence of vision. Cyberous interaction with the self's nervous system will begin at ever earlier ages with ever increasing intrusion. The path is there to see.

We began with precocious teens using their parents' desktop computers, then laptops and notebooks; the introduction of computers in high schools; then elementary schools. Laptops and notebooks became required in science classes. Cellphones and Personal Digital Assistants merged into smartphones. Smartphones moved down from early adopter adults to become commonplace among teens, and now elementary school children. The iPad and its many imitators have trickled down to preschoolers. Three-year-olds are now using their 'pads' to 'surf' children's stories and whatever on the web. Toddlers are trained by 'toys' that respond to their actions (there is that 'regime of competence' again) and encourage them to interact. Six-month-olds are lulled to sleep, or wakefulness, with displays projected on the ceiling. Do we access the womb next? These systems will engage the immature self in accelerated and intensive self-organization affecting early residual neural patterns shaping the self for life. Cyber augmented post-birth development, extending throughout life, will be insidious—in the guise of the next 'fun' interface, or the next productivity tool, or the next social network, or whatever collaborative minds create for interaction with collaborative minds. Hierarchies will build relentlessly.

These experiences will be instilled in the most basic residual patterns of our nervous systems: patterns that will be standing ready to participate in subsequent disturbances, precipitating new resonances, and new sudden insights, and enriching metaphorical thinking. The modalities of these cyberous augmentations will contribute to the emergence of mind through our interaction and registration, through the residual patterns they will collaboratively self-organize in our neuronal systems. The participation of cyberous collaborations in order to finesse the unknowable will be increasingly and routinely reinforced by culture—and be increasingly and routinely unknowable.

It is in this post-birth-development-driven cyberous augmentation that we will find, literally, the new mind's eye—reaching out to new resources having alien modalities. Or will the environment reach in seeking new sources?

Is this realistic? Today we have YouTube, Facebook and scores of wannabees gathering the experiences of millions of augmented eyes. Web sites with stationary cameras provide views of both real-time excitement and the humdrum. Today human observers search and register what those cameras 'see.' Tomorrow? Pattern recognition algorithms will evaluate the multiple sources for patterns and present the 'images' of what *matters* to whomever or whatever, whenever, and wherever… for use in multiple scales and modalities. Just as with the Facebook photo 'tag,' algorithms for recognizing and presenting patterns from molecular to cosmological, from friend or stranger—the images will participate in the self-organization of the mind. The post-birth experience of cyberous culture will prepare us.

Let us not forget what we set aside earlier in this chapter: that which falls in the crease between the unknowable, that is beyond human experience, and that which is unknown but of 'me', the thin line where we find the ahaa and the metaphor. Our own systems, like the young mothers at the mall, will collaborate with the unknowable and make it ours. Future generations will not know the difference. We don't today!

The Sounds of Mind

While the translations of alien modalities are achieved principally through vision, the sounds of mind continue to permeate our culture, the exchanges among ourselves—and within ourselves. What will be the consequences of the intense visual translation of alien modalities to the sounds of mind? Will we stop talking to one another? Not anytime soon. We share experience through sound.

What we see today must be named or described with sounds of words. The patterns stimulated through the interaction of sight and the environment self-organize with identifying tags of sound. 'Primitive' tribes culturally taught to perceive and describe only two colors—green and not green—demonstrate that the words of culture and the sounds of mind can impose constraints on cognition! If you learn there is only a sound for green and a sound for not green, you cannot then think of something as red. There is no red in your culture. There is no 'red' in your sounds of mind.

Two aspects of sound will channel the future of the mind. First, words are an interface for transferring ideas, and organizing among members of a culture—the custodians of post-birth development. The sounds of words are integral elements in the residual patterns of concepts. As the sounds of mind, they are elements in the residual patterns of self, participating in the processes of cognition.

Second, sounds have a pre-eminence in post-birth development that continues through life. The sounds of words—of mind—seem to be the neuronal last mile, the slow bottleneck of transmission! But are they really? While the sounds themselves may move slowly, the vast amounts of information encoded in sounds is without parallel. Consider a 'black hole,' or a 'quark.' To cosmologists or physicists, incredible stores of information and memory, of research and observation, of analyses and conclusions are bundled and ready for action with a single word—a literal puff of air. Consider 'peach.' That word conjures up unique color ('peachy' is itself a zip file of description), fuzzy yet firm to the touch, a juicy and sweet taste, and likely a pleasant memory or two—maybe even a gentle breeze in warm sunlight. Or, consider that Google crawler of a few paragraphs back. With 'crawler' we have zip-filed an entire unknowable phenomenon in one puff of air. In mind those sounds sit waiting not only for normal use, but for the unexpected exigency of metaphor.

Images are shared with the patterns of sound. They are given meaning— tagged—with sounds. The expression of mind for interacting within ourselves and among others is still integrated with the residual patterns of sound. The sounds of mind will likely be accommodated in this future of mind. And yet there are hints of change: the simplest are the emoticons of the keyboard— ;>). And what might become of the posting of images as updates or responses on social networks?

The Self, That Subjective Realm

There are two 'selfs' of interest here. The ones we know—me, you, us; and the ones we may have created.

First, me. The self-organizing subjective realm integrates the current physical state of 'me' with the registration of environmental disturbances of 'not me,' providing an inventory of residual patterns for comparison, resonance, recognition, and meaning. The subjective realm is essential to pattern recognition and to cognition. Meaning is to me. The meaning of a disturbance, the registration, is with respect to the residual patterns of a CAS—me. The translation of alien modalities and the mysterious travels of the crawler may increase the unknowable, but the translations impinging on the boundaries of me will still be subject to the self-organizations of patterns reflecting the current physical state of me and environmental disturbances to 'me.' An increase in the unknowable will not change that. It will change the extent to which the self matters to mind. As the unknowable becomes an increasing source of mind, as sources beyond the limits of human experience become more influential to the emergence of mind, self will be less of an influential element in the emergence of that mind.

Now, what about those selfs we may be creating? Our considerations of pattern-recognition-based cognitions, our theories of mind, focus on a mind constrained to the individual. We must re-perceive the subjective realm in a context that is not limited by the body. The self of the body may not be as significant to the whole. Corporeal selfs may not be alone.

What am I saying? That there is a subjective realm that is not unique to self, to *me, you,* or *us.* That there are other 'references of experience,' sets of residual patterns available for resonance and recognition, apart from *me, you,* or *us. They are cyberous.* Today, histories are assembled in the records, files, observations, algorithms, actions and consequences of cyberous systems. Our friendly crawler and its compatriots of similar design continuously add to that experience. These 'learned' experiences are available in synthetic memory for comparison, resonance, and action. Do they provide a basis for meaning? They invoke responses by the systems using them. Patterns registered by these cyberous systems, patterns resonating with residual patterns, are meaningful to the systems in which they are stored. The systems respond, they take action on them. Humphrey, in *A History of The Mind* said, "I feel therefore I am!" Is that essential to self? Must systems 'feel' in order to be subjective realms? There is meaning without feeling. A cyberous self is an adjacent possibility. We will explore this further in Chapter 15.

Into the Unknowable

This is not a future of the mind we will celebrate. It will likely be a slow slide through adjacent possibilities unheralded by any grand or discernible phase shift on the human time scale. The changes already underway will continue to be relatively gradual, yet cumulatively profound. Can this really happen?

There are six factors signaling that this future of the mind is in progress:

- First, our neuronal systems are *collaboratively* self-organizing with cyberous systems.

- Secondly, mind is already an emergence of environmental systems *and* neural ones: it is as much a function of an increasingly cyberous environment as it is of self.

- Thirdly, our species' post-birth development prepares us to collaborate with whatever environment we find ourselves in, including one increasingly complex, visually oriented, and cyber augmented.

- Fourthly, the power and influence of cyberous collaboration and alien modalities is due to a remarkably facile relationship with vision—one that we create and encourage.

- Fifthly, the augmenting resources for pattern recognition now include disturbances and self-organizations occurring *within* the synthetic environment, interpreted for our neuronal systems by cyberous ones. These systems use techniques which present analyses, results, patterns, and consequences to us from phenomena beyond the limits of human experience!

- Lastly, there is today a continuing increase in the hierarchies of self-organization of our own systems in collaboration with those that are not ours. As the elements available for this self-organization become richer, unknown layers emerge. The process provides new layers of self-organization, new residual patterns for recognition and response, new sources for the emergence of 'my' mind and yours. Disbelief? Consider the person you would be if you had never seen or used your electronic accoutrements—your laptop or iPad, MP3 or iPod, your smartphone.

Mind is becoming the emergence of a greater number of elements and ensuing hierarchies, themselves emergent and unknowable. We are not likely to be aware of the difference—except as the usual generation gap distinguishing youth as more quickly accepting of the new, while the elders hesitate or fail completely!

Suggested Additional Reading for Chapter 13

Alva Noe, in *Out of Our Heads: Why You Are Not Your Brain, and Other Lessons from the Biology of Consciousness*, explores the concept of an extended mind, the aspects of mind contributing to its being unknowable, and suggests alternatives to the brain-mind dichotomy of the last two hundred years.

Nicholas Humphrey, in *A History of the Mind*, discusses the importance of boundaries and modalities to the self and to mind, and provides a fundamental perspective of 'me' and 'not me,' exposing the intrinsic nature of the subjective realm. Antonio Damasio, in *Descartes' Error,* discusses the underlying processes of the mind, those of which we do not know.

In *The Fundamentals of Brain Development*, Joan Stiles integrates a discussion of biology and environment at several levels of development from the molecular to cognition.

Andy Clark's *Supersizing the Mind* examines the present integration of external systems with internal neural systems, and explores the distinction between an environment simply augmenting neural systems and one that collaborates with them, inducing the emergence of mind.

CHAPTER 14
An Absentee Mind

What in our lives—in 'me' today—suggests a mind that is partly 'absent?' How much of what you think you know is really in your head? How much would you actually know if you were unable to access those gadgets you have? A report in the July 15, 2011 issue of *Science* is suggestive. Titled "Searching for the Google Effect in People's Memories," the research suggested that people relying on Google to find information remembered how to find the information... but not the information itself. The implication is that if the search process were not available the information would not be either. Yet, these study subjects would likely claim to 'know about it' if they were asked. This isn't absent-mindedness, it is absent mind. That's what this chapter is about: the systems participating in the emergence of mind that are not *of* 'me' and the implications to 'me.'

As with the unknowable mind, it can be argued that this is nothing new. And it isn't... yet it is! We have been using external memory for millennia. Einstein once said "Never memorize what you can look up in books." So what is different about silicon? Is it simply a matter of degree? Is cyberous augmentation simply an extension of the past? Cyberous augmentation is more intense, more insidious, and more collaborative.

That was not always so. Mobility was the game changer. When cyberous interfaces became mobile, when they jumped into our pockets to be with us wherever and forever, not only did cyberous augmentation change, so did our sensuous interfaces and expectations. The augmentations offered by the desktop computer, the TV set, or that old fashioned movie screen were fixed—nailed to the floor so to speak. We went to them like the ancient Greeks went to Delphi... or we were not augmented. It was necessary to seek out cyberous augmentation. Now, the cyberous is a constant companion.

Synthetic augmentation of the senses has assumed extraordinary importance in humans. As synthetic augmentation of the central nervous system increases and becomes even more integrated, and as post-birth development becomes more attuned to the character of these augmentations, environmental elements will multiply in number and increase in significance. However much you may feel otherwise, your smartphone, iPad, or other devices are not part of you. These elements are part of 'not me.' They are in every sense absent from 'me.' These cyberous systems of 'not me' have become significant in the collaboration that gives rise to mind.

We have traced the history of mind in order to identify trajectories for projecting into the future. That history suggests that the neural systems of the body have not changed over the last 50,000 years. The resources of the central nervous system remain much as they were when the second diaspora began out of Africa, 50–100,000 years ago. Despite a significant increase in the total neural resources of the brain about 500,000 years ago, indications are that little change has taken place in the basic *organization* since then. Instead, the crucial move into adjacent possibilities has been through intensified internal interconnectedness of the neural systems, and intensified interaction with environmental systems. The principal forces operating in this future of mind will be pattern recognition—the residual patterns of remote systems collaborating with neural systems.

Cyberous Systems

Let's return to that Google search. It takes place on the other side of the interface defining 'me.' Where? Who knows? More importantly, who cares? The source of the collaboration introduced to me at my boundary is unequivocally 'not me.' The interfaces we have created finesse whatever concerns we may initially have. They are too easy, too transparent to matter.

The Web itself has rules for interaction that transcend any culture we may occupy. The multitude of systems, data sources, modalities, and analyses follow the rules of wherever they are... outside of 'me.' Yet the Web itself is only a fraction of what lies out there. The Internet, on which the Web hitches a ride, is described as having a hierarchy of four interacting layers. The collaboration of the elements of the Web add to that. Those new smartphone 'apps' also ride the Internet, adding still more remote layers and complexity. Now the 'Cloud' seems to have trumped them all in remoteness. Its advocates tell us to put it all out there. Somewhere. All of our personal records, the memories in photographs and videos, anything we have digitized for convenience should be out there—not just outside of me, but outside of the gadgets that have become part of me. Even the software, the rules for obtaining the material we put out there—even that should be out there. Plato's shadows on the wall of a cave have nothing on the Cloud.

The Google crawler registers only some of the Web's self-organizations. The other self-organizations go unnoticed by man or machine and the residual patterns of much that augments 'me' are lost to us. Yet, we have no sense of remoteness. There are even times when we become so transparently immersed we are unaware of the boundaries between the cyberous and our 'selfs.'

And yet those seductive systems on the other side of the boundary that is 'me' are collaborating in the emergence of the mind of 'me.' The patterns, the parsing and translating, the modalities, all of that experience I have not had on the other side of the boundary, all of it is collaborating in the emergence of the mind of 'me'—remotely.

The elements of the central nervous system do not very well discern distinctions between disturbances of the natural world and those brought to them by synthetic augmentations. We may 'know' our senses are being stimulated by a smartphone display, but does that matter functionally to the emergent mind? How many of us have become so immersed in that screen, or some other cyberous stimulation, that we become unaware of our natural surroundings—the 'window of life'?

There is more to a sense than the simple impact of a disturbance registering on the distant edges of the neural system. There are residual neural patterns reaching out to encompass many other elements of the neural system for support in recognition and response. Today, neural systems reach out through the modalities of synthetic augmentations to the environment as well. We cannot overestimate the power and influence of augmenting cyberous systems on the development of neural connectivity and interaction.

Post-Birth Development

Hominids have excelled in the use of post-birth development as a means for adapting to otherwise inhospitable niches. We are opportunists. Post-birth development has in turn shaped its own container—culture. Culture, the intimate 'not me,' now dominates the post-birth development of 'me.'

It is in the emergence of culture and its capacity for creating, incubating, and transmitting non-life-dependent forms, that the sensuous interfaces enabling the augmentation of the senses have blossomed. Collections of neural systems—groups of people in cultures—nurture these interfaces like workers surrounding a queen bee. Equally important to culture are the cyberous artifacts, the remotely resident 'apps' that are always there to shape us and inform us.

Consider the implications of this collaboration—the parallel self-organization of our sensuous interfaces, and post-birth development as our environment. The accoutrements of culture have changed through a sequence of adjacent possibilities from those needed for group living and survival to the cyber synthetic augmentations of the senses and the cyber-neural collaboration that is coalescing within us today. The need for group living is being subsumed by the urge to explore the adjacent possibilities of collaboration with remote, absent, cyberous systems: systems that are not *of* 'me.'

Post-birth development continues to nurture this absentee relationship:

- We are shaped by systems of 'not me' which are designed to extend the raw material for the emergence of mind residing in 'not me.'

- Each new app, each task delegated to the cyberous 'not me,' grooms us for the next one, increasing the collaboration of 'not me' in the mind of 'me.'

- The original 'regime of competency,' culture presents ever more complex challenges and rewards for collaboration with remote systems absent from 'me.'

- Synthetic augmentations have enabled the collaboration of alien systems in mind—systems in every sense absent from 'me.'

Vision

Vision has become an unknowing accomplice with these systems. The systems underlying vision are most open to augmentation for collaboration with remote systems. The most powerful, influential, and voracious user of neuronal systems—vision—has extended its domain far beyond the systems of sight. As with the Bay Bridge, we might ask—where does vision begin, where does it end? Where does its insatiable appetite for support and collaboration end? Where does its influence not persist? Vision leads our journey into the cyber collaboration with the central nervous system of which it is a part.

The neuronal systems enabling vision have an extraordinary capability for self-organizing and are powerfully adept at pattern acquisition and recognition. As we saw in Chapter 6, this self-organizing is particularly powerful in infants. Even as we marvel at the power and influence of vision, our culture works to increase its influence on pattern acquisition and recognition, metaphor and... cognition. Most importantly, the systems and interfaces giving emergence to vision thrive on the extended, far-flung, alien augmentations of 'not me' that we unite with 'me.' The emergence of vision seems to thrive on the stimulation of absentee collaborative systems.

Pattern Recognition

The cyberous extension of vision opens exciting new playgrounds for our irresistible search for patterns. Just as the patterns of today's culture would be incomprehensible to our ancestors of 50,000 years ago—even 5,000 years ago—so too will the patterns commonly acquired in this future confound us because the synthetic augmentations of our post-birth development offer quite different experiences than those of our ancestors—and those our descendants will have. Vision, learned in the post-birth incubator of culture, is acutely sensitive to patterns of 'not me.'

What ever-so-slight alteration in the body's neuronal elements might begin changes that qualitatively alter the whole basis for acquisition and interpretation of patterns? Will the systems underlying vision develop multiple schemes of registration enabling us to focus on multiple inputs simultaneously? Or will the neuronal self-organizations and collaborations supporting vision further divide the pattern registration originating in sight, giving us multiple, simultaneous understanding of what we 'see?' We should expect new development as these systems test adjacent possibilities for self-organization.

Yet pattern acquisition is not the real story here: it is metaphor and its power in cognition. The patterns experienced through the collaboration of absentee cyberous and neuronal elements—alien, cyberous experience from 'not me' that collaborates with 'me' in the emergence of mind—will incalculably extend metaphor's support of cognition. Pattern recognition and metaphor will flourish in ways we have little hope of understanding. They will be supported by systems of 'not me,' absentee systems.

Sounds or Not

We have explored how the sounds of mind echo our thoughts and encapsulate the very concepts of mind. Will they limit this future of mind? Not likely.

Both vision and the sounds of mind are bases for metaphor and cognition. Each has its own systems for supporting the processes of cognition. As with all elemental systems of the mind, they overlap in multiple, shifting self-organizations. The sounds of mind may inhibit the expression of visual metaphor, not because their systems become more dominant, but because visual metaphors become so enriched that they become increasingly beyond the capability of the sounds of mind to express or communicate. Perhaps the shared experience underlying the communications of all metaphors will still suffice. The expressions "crash and burn" and "she had a meltdown" would have been unintelligible as characterizations of states of mind a thousand years ago—even a hundred years ago. But does it matter? Experience, even remote or absentee experience, will likely be conceptualized by the economies of the sounds of mind.

Then again, maybe not. The limitations of expression by the sounds of mind may redirect the means of expression. The persistence of the sounds of mind into the future of mind coupled with cyberous systems giving emergence to vision could open adjacent possibilities beyond our imagination.

Metaphor will continue on a path of enrichment... but the mind may experience some constraining force. Perhaps visual-based metaphors, inhibited by the sounds of mind, will emerge through some unknowable aspect of mind—as in the mysterious process of ahaa!

Culture will be under the pressure of adjacent possibilities to release the power of these suppressed visual metaphors through additional augmentation. This future would then be subject even more to the development of sensuous augmentation, to the accoutrements of culture.

A mind without its sounds seems incomprehensible. The sounds of mind, the zip files of cognition, are not likely to cease. The sounds of mind will not forestall self-organization into the adjacent possibility of an absentee mind.

The Future of Subjective-ness

What is the role of self in this future? What happens to me in the absentee mind?

The systems of self will maintain their residuals. Body states and functions will remain an important part of the residual patterns of self. They will continue participating in the emergence of mind and they will continue to be important to me.

But 'me' will be less important to mind. The subjective realm will persist, but self—those residual body states and residual patterns of body functions, those definers of 'me' and the present—will diminish in power and influence as the absentee cyberous elements self-organize in their own domains, with their own modalities—in an increasingly absentee mind. If the self-organization of remote systems collaborates in the emergence of my mind, it matters less if I am asleep, in pain, hungry, or in love. Have you ever emerged from an intense session with the cyberous and suddenly realized you are cold or hungry? My smartphone downloads, updates, authenticates, and notifies while I am doing all of these other things… and it does it without 'me.' Self may even become dependent on residual patterns reflecting states extending into the cyberous domain, or from the cyberous domain into self. The external systems will register disturbances to them such as network or sub-system failures, overloads, or errors of one kind or another. These conditions will be reflected in the self—loss of memory or function. Texting and Twitter already reach into the residual patterns of self, bringing with them residual patterns and conditions of the 'not me.'

We glimpse this in the social websites of today, too. Cyberous systems already collaborate in the residuals of self. The self today incorporates the states of cyberous residual patterns and interactions… even to the point of inducing bodily reactions like depression, joy, and suicide. There are almost daily reports of children subjected to cyberous bullying, of people reacting to online abuse, or seduced by social site excesses, or spam. This will be a difficult trip for the ego.

A Diaspora of Systems

Any sequence of sensuous interfaces opens onto still more adjacent possibilities. Each step in the sequence positions us for the next. The sequence of initial states and sets of adjacent possibilities has been crucial to where we are today and will go in the future.

Today, the mind emerges from countless neuronal and environmental elements coalescing in shifting relationships increasingly dispersed throughout a limitless artificial environment. Consider the countless components behind a simple web search, the unknown hierarchies of systems, the unknowable relationships of these systems to the typical user, the ease of information acquisition... and the yet-to-be-discovered self-organizing patterns among them. Or return to the daily life of the smartphone and how *it* so obligingly *includes you* in its busy life of self-organization.

The physical and knowledge-integrating nature of these systems (do cyberous systems themselves have culture?) stimulates influences, structures and architectures, intentions and designs far beyond the boundaries of 'me.' Yet, a timely response for 'me' in a time of need is all that is necessary for these systems to participate with 'me' in the experiences of the subjective self and the emergence of mind.

The operation of culture is more subtle than a computer game, but no less relentless in its push to extend the skill of our collaboration with artifacts of its own creation, with remote systems. We have examined several sequentially developed interfaces for use between our neural system and the environment—each interface enables self-organizing at a unique point through adjacent possibilities, offering an appropriate level of competency and rewards. Each new augmenting interface offers interaction and complexity that extend earlier interfaces, yet each incorporates simple rules for exchange with 'me:' GPS systems coaxing us through alien countryside and 'Sirius' supporting us with (usually) timely advice and information. Each small step further reducing the importance of proximity for collaboration. Each successive cultural regime of competency promotes spatially more widely distributed, absentee systems for collaboration in the emergence of mind.

Non-Resident Emigrants

For all of their importance to the emergence of mind, these cyberous elements are not resident in the central nervous system. We seldom know where they do reside—or even if there is a physical location for them as they move across the 'me' and 'not me' boundary. This is a crucial dimension to the emergence of mind. These cyberous elements are absent from the central nervous system, yet interface with the self and participate in the emergence of mind. In the absence of these environmental elements the mind would be of an entirely different qualitative nature. Go ahead, throw away your smartphone!

This absentee dimension underlying the emergence of mind opens profound adjacent possibilities: the elements giving rise to the mind are not limited to those we find in the natural world; memory is no longer constrained by the number and organization of neurons; knowledge is no longer limited to individual experience; cognition is no longer limited to 'me.' Once the nervous system became more integrally linked with its environment, once absentee elements began participating more intensely in the stimulation of systems underlying the emergence of mind, the potential character of those absentee elements became limitless in adjacent possibilities. Each state of the cyberous, that vast web of augmentation with its own elements and self-organization, is exposed to an incredible number of adjacent possibilities and disruptions.

What is the personal side of all of this absentee collaboration? What does it mean to 'me?' A web site crash, a network overload, a sloppy upgrade by a systems operator, a software upgrade missed, disabling malware—each of these deprive 'me' of functionality, knowledge, and memory. Each of these can be paralyzing to 'me.' Cyberous 'strokes,' disruptions or failures of 'not me,' are becoming as serious to 'me' as the biological ones *of* 'me.' The increasingly unknowable mind of the last chapter may be so familiar as to be unnoticed. It is a journey through adjacent possibilities we may recognize and understand. The absentee mind is another matter. Will it still be mine? And who—or what is 'me?'

Suggested Additional Reading for Chapter 14

Andy Clark's *Supersizing the Mind* examines the present integration of external systems with internal neural systems, and explores the distinction between an environment simply augmenting neural systems and one that collaborates with them, inducing the emergence of mind.

Nicholas Humphrey, in *A History of the Mind,* discusses the importance of boundaries and modalities to the self and to mind, and provides a fundamental perspective of 'me' and 'not me,' exposing the intrinsic nature of the subjective realm.

The July 2013 issue of IEEE's publication, *Computer*, explores a current development in the visual collaboration of 'me' and the cyberous 'not me' in the field of Visual analytics.

Two books provide perspectives from opposite sides of the cyberous-culture/mind interface. Adam Greenfield, in *Everyware: the Dawning Age of Ubiquitous Computing*, explores contemporary cyberous systems influencing and participating in the evolution of the mind. Gary Small and Gigi Vorgan in *iBrain: Surviving the Technological Alteration of the Modern Mind*, review generational differences in adaptation to the cyberous culture.

CHAPTER 15
The Transcendent Mind

*"The light! From beneath me—inside the Earth—shining upward, through the rocks,
the ground, everything—growing brighter, brighter, blinding—"*

In his conclusion to *Childhood's End*, Arthur C. Clarke, in a self-transforming, towering web of energy that consumes the Earth itself, has mankind join the Overmind, an unimaginable fusion of minds from across the universe. Did he get it right again as he has so often? Mind, as an emergent property of CASs, themselves comprised of numerous independent interacting elements of virtually any description, is open to adjacent possibilities we may find incomprehensible. We characterize this third potential future of mind as transcendent. What is that? A transcendent mind is one that is higher than our individual minds in the hierarchy of emergence. Now that sounds spooky, doesn't it, or perhaps a little sci-fi? To our subjective realms it is preposterous, perhaps threatening. But is Clarke's future constrained to fiction?

Ironically, and perhaps counter-intuitively, it is within the trajectory of post-birth development that we will find the transcendent mind. Cyberous culture, shaping our post-birth development, will prepare us to participate in this mind.

The first two futures we have explored are still personal. This third future of mind will not only be beyond our comprehension, beyond our knowing, but beyond self. Undertaking the exploration of this potential future of mind is ambitious at the least and arrogant at most. While changes in pattern recognition, vision, and post-birth development—the continuums of adjacent possibilities—point in the direction of a transcendent mind, the principal re-perception required for imagining this future of mind is context. We must stretch still further the context of what gives rise to this thing we call mind.

Within the process of change, within CASs, there is no specific limitation to the self-organizing hierarchies of CASs or properties emerging from them. Only initial conditions limit the adjacent possibilities of change.

Consider:

- Patterns are not unique to those modalities registered by our sensuous interfaces. Patterns registered by alien modalities are translated and presented to us by our interfaces with the cyberous.

- Pattern recognition is not unique to human systems.

- Vision is increasingly emerging from collaborating cyberous systems through augmenting interfaces. This is presenting adjacent possibilities for exploration that are beyond our comprehension.

- Post-birth development is increasingly under the influence of cyberous systems. The "self," the subjective realm, is increasingly *of* cyberous systems.

The increasing independence and self-organizing capacities of collaborating cyberous systems will provide us with a continuing post-birth experience facilitating our *participation* in the emergence of mind. We are being prepared to participate.

Really? What suggests such a future of the mind? In Chapter 3 we introduced Damasio's definition of emotion as a combination of mental evaluation with dispositional bodily response. If we substitute cyberous for mental and system for bodily we open some interesting possibilities.

In scenario planning it is often useful to look for early indicators, developments that are suggestive of the emergence of a particular series of events or a 'future.' A report in the September 30, 2011 issue of *Science* is suggestive. Social scientists have used an analysis of the words contained in Twitter messages to study the collective moods of millions of people in diverse cultures around the world. It seems that Twitter has a 'mood,' that is to say, feelings. Or is it the collective of Twitter users—the 'body' of Twitter—that has feelings? Other social media have been used to study the movement of information, 'persuasion,' and events such as the 'Arab Spring' uprisings. The authors suggest that these are the changing moods of humanity—not simply the collective feeling of millions of individuals. As discussed in Chapter 3, 'feelings' are a manifestation of a subjective realm, a self. Perhaps the computer virus Flame is also a suggestive early indicator. It is composed of many distinct modules that self-organize as a unit. Each module operates independently but success is a product of the collective, the whole. No individual part succeeds alone. The virus has the ability to impersonate legitimate programs as well as users, and takes over control of infected computers. But what makes it of interest as an early indicator are its abilities. Once resident in a computer, without prompting, it will monitor in-boxes, capture screen presentations, remotely turn on microphones, and capture conversations happening near the computer— and numerous other things, essentially replacing the user. And to top it off, it is heuristic: it learns and takes action on what it learns. Early indicators do not guarantee anything. They are simply factors that suggest the potential emergence of a future. Yet, they *are* suggestive.

How are these early indicators suggestive of the emergence of a transcendent mind? The first, Twitter, is suggestive of a self-organizing system comprised of multiple interacting cultures, which are in turn comprised of numerous interacting individual minds—a layered system registering and responding to a stimulus in the environment. The second, Flame, is suggestive of a self-organizing system registering stimulations in the environment, recognizing patterns and taking action based on experience. Both are systems that transcend their basic elements. Both are systems with the potential for emergent properties.

Transcendent mind has profound implications for the subjective realm, the self. Could we claim this mind as ours? Would it claim us? What are the implications to transcendent mind of the three trajectories we have identified: pattern recognition, vision, and post-birth development? Pattern recognition and the subjective realm is a good place to begin.

Pattern Recognition and the Subjective Realm

Patterns have brought us a long way. Pattern recognition is as old as life itself. Pattern recognition is the bedrock of survival, the mother of metaphor, and metaphor is a language of cognition.

As we proceed here, we can have less confidence in the assertion of our answers to the questions posed—even of the questions themselves. The perplexity arising from the limits of the very systems we use for acquisition, registration and recognition imprison our efforts to respond to the very questions we raise. The questions themselves may seem absurd. Yet there do not seem to be limitations on systems other than our own for registering and recognizing patterns.

Pattern recognition requires residual patterns, or some record of what was before, as a basis for recognition; experience requires registration; and registration requires a place that matters—a subjective realm, what is happening to me. Our place that matters, our reference for pattern recognition, begins with 'me' and 'not me.' If the registration of patterns requires a subjective realm, is there a subjective realm transcending our own?

Even more alien to the self, could a subjective realm be established with a 'canned' history, outfitted by other sources—without actually 'living' a prior interaction? If so, would it be adequately subjective and nimbly available for the operation of metaphor? Many of our own histories, our own 'experiences' from which we interact and respond are not our own. They are canned and provided to us by families, tribes, and cultures, through post-birth development. Today many are provided by cyberous systems.

Our subjective realm is one scheme of pattern recognition. Can we claim the recognition of patterns to be uniquely our own capability? Hardly. We have invented technologies to translate patterns recognized by alien modalities. Would a subjective realm even be part of this transcendent emergence? The study of the moods of Twitter suggests that it would. Feelings are the direct perception of the body's landscape—what's going on with 'me?' The moods identified by this study of Twitter are the sensing of the landscape represented by the body of tweets—the landscape of the collective participants as a single system. While the references to 'me' and our collective 'selfs' will not disappear, they may inhibit our awareness of this emergence. Today, post-birth development, culture, and experience establish a collective reference of 'us'—families, interest groups, institutions, political states—a more collaborative perspective is beyond the comprehension of most of us. Cyberous systems have the prerequisites for a subjective realm.

But there are threads in the exploration of patterns and pattern recognition that are useful:

- The existence of patterns in the environment does not depend on recognition by *our* nervous system. We already translate patterns in alien modalities into familiar ones.

- *Our* basis for pattern recognition is not a unique phenomenon. Alien modalities do just fine!

- The response of a cyberous system to disturbance is not qualitatively different than our own. It registers stimulation and has associated, predisposed responses—emotions?

- There are likely already patterns of disturbances and responses *we* are unable to perceive as patterns—even with synthetic augmentation.

Let's elaborate on these points.

The existence of patterns in the environment does not depend on recognition by our nervous system.

Our recognition of patterns does not bestow some hitherto-unearned set of credentials on them. We design synthetic augmenting systems for the sole purpose of registering patterns of modalities in the environment that our nervous systems cannot discern. These systems are also capable of discerning similarities as presented in different contexts, in different media, and in different times and places. These systems are capable of learning from experience. The very term pattern recognition arises from these design efforts. The patterns can be registered and used by whatever capability comes along. In fact the value of these systems is that they function in our absence, and in modalities we do not perceive.

Our basis for pattern recognition is not a unique phenomenon.

Our process of pattern recognition involves sensation, perception, and resonance with what we previously registered—the residual patterns of self. Inherent in this process is an element of subjectivity: what is happening to 'me.'

Residual patterns are established in synthetic systems. Synthetic systems interact with and register disturbances in the environment. They evaluate what is happening to the system, to 'me.' There are consequences that follow the registrations. In that sense there is a 'known' history of what has happened to 'me.' Our process of registration and patterns recognition is not unique.

The response of a cyberous system to disturbance is not qualitatively different than our own.

We have experience with life systems comprised of more than the individual, more than just 'me:' groups, societies, cultures. Are there other realms of meaning? Consider our working definitions of self, consciousness, and mind. As we have used them, they are emergent properties of the interaction of elements in a system. There are other emergences of which we are unaware. Our own collective activities foment emergences, as do the synthetic systems collaborating with us.

There are likely already patterns of disturbances and responses we are unable to perceive as patterns—even with synthetic augmentation.

The theory of CASs gives us no reason to think otherwise. We have already seen that there are patterns of recurring disturbances which are completely alien to registration by our systems—from black holes to quarks; there are probably also disturbances which we cannot even design augmenting systems to detect. Why should it not be so? Our capacities are a product of long continuums, of slipping and sliding through initial conditions and adjacent possibilities. That is not unique. We may wish to be unique, but it does not follow from what we have explored.

As our systems self-organized to register disturbances, and coupled responses to those disturbances, initial conditions and adjacent possibilities were explored, and by implication, others were not. The others are not of our subjective realm. Yet, there is no reason to preclude the existence of alternative patterns to those we are capable of registering simply because the explorations of adjacent possibilities by our self-organizations did not include them.

What of Metaphor?

Metaphor is *of* pattern recognition. What exactly must we re-perceive in metaphor? This is a difficult re-perception, for the entire concept of metaphor is subjective, experiential, and must have a shared basis. Without some degree of shared experience, metaphor cannot be communicated. We have already seen that characteristics among patterns can have commonality with one another in different dimensions or constructs. These characteristics of commonality are adaptable for enhancing understanding of new patterns encountered. Do cyberous systems have the prerequisites for the use of metaphor?

Metaphor is inherently ambiguous in that some indefinable degree of commonality, some set of entailments, must exist in both the subject and the reference. Yet, there cannot be so many commonalities as to be simply a repetition, or so few commonalities as to lack any basis for shared understanding. Metaphor is arbitrary, too, in that it selectively highlights similarities while ignoring dissimilarities. Metaphor is unpredictable in that it arises from contexts and experiences so different as to be illogical—and from processes not knowable. How do we re-perceive metaphor?

There is some unknowable process by which what is revealed is separated from what is hidden in our experience of metaphor. Metaphor is *of* human experience. But the process is certainly unknown. Metaphor seems to operate at some level of self-organization beneath that which gives emergence to mind. The subjective experience—the residual patterns—form the basis of meaning, and shared residual patterns are the basis of metaphor.

Residual patterns of experience can be designed, constructed, and made available for resonance. A 'database' of experience, of residual patterns, can be constructed for response to external disturbance. Today, cyberous systems can operate with degrees of ambiguity, be selective and precise, yet be inclusive, identify characteristics in one circumstance, and use them in another.

There may be alternatives to the prerequisites defined as necessary for the operation of metaphor, but will we understand them? If each of these prerequisites of metaphor—residual patterns, registration, and subjective reference—achieves a cyberous, collaborative basis, will there be a basis for metaphor? Without an understanding of the processes of metaphor we cannot know. Can these systems exercise the requisite simultaneous ambiguity and precision of metaphor? We have no reason to preclude these adjacent possibilities.

Our cyberous collaborators bring us experiences for use in metaphor. Search engines bring results, experiences, to us, and to others. Metaphor 'entailments' are in the assembled results—fodder for metaphor. Do our cyberous collaborators use metaphor? They are of a subjective realm. Can these systems exercise the requisite simultaneous ambiguity and precision of metaphor? We are not likely to know, but we have no reason to preclude those adjacent possibilities.

Vision

What is the importance of vision in this future of the mind? Vision will still be an essential interface for the emergence of our mind, but our mind is not the issue here. What role will vision play in the emergence of the transcendent mind? Vision will be important in the emergence of the transcendent mind for two reasons. First, it will continue to be important to the emergence of our minds and our minds will be among the simple elements interacting and collaborating with the cyberous in the emergence of the transcendent mind. Secondly, as we have moved through adjacent possibilities, jointly and collaboratively with cyberous systems, we have favored cyberous systems compatible with vision. We are equipping cyberous systems with vision. Let's review vision before elaborating. We must re-perceive vision, too.

An emergent property, vision, arises from the collaboration of sight and other systems in our central nervous system, and systems of the external environment. Vision is pattern recognition. Vision is *of* a subjective realm. It is learned. Vision, emerging from a vast range of residual patterns, from a multitude of collaborating systems, organizes experience—the resonance of current perception and the residual patterns of prior self-organizations. All of these things begin with sight and sight is no longer constrained to the biological.

Today, sight is augmented by systems alien to our subjective realm by humanly contrived systems which artificially extend our capabilities. Patterns different in nature or character than those registered by our own systems are translated, learned, and recognized through the interface of sight and the emergence of vision. The interfaces we design smooth the self-organizing of alien disturbances and patterns within our own. Furthermore, considerable self-organization and analysis takes place in these systems before anything is shared with us—perhaps an emergence that is not of 'me.'

Is there a vision beyond the experience of our subjective realm? Is there a collective vision—an institutional vision, or a cultural vision? Must vision 'see' as we do? Is our participation even required for the emergence of properties having the characteristics we label vision? Can vision emerge from cyberous sources alone? The answer to all of these questions is yes. The adjacent possibilities are there. An entire industry works to have robots 'see' and respond to what they 'see.' The uniqueness of vision's self-organization is sight. The systems we have designed with interfaces to 'see' self-organize with the sight—the registrations—we have given them, and respond.

Reports of unintended consequences in the design of cyberous systems are not uncommon. Interfaces meld and mesh cyberous protocols, obscuring the unintended—perhaps unknowable consequences. The consequences of connections and rules for interactions among the vast number of these cyberous systems are beyond our knowledge. We can speculate. What of those video cameras we discussed in Chapter 12, those active in the detection of a public safety threat in New York City in 2010, the video postings on social networks, the 'sights' monitored by web sites? What if they had been interconnected with an algorithm to collaborate not only with one another but with augmenting information systems and response mechanisms? What if they were all just waiting for that algorithm to be released with intended or perhaps unintended consequences of cyberous vision? Is this the equivalent of the cyberous multiple eye of the fly? Are there fly-like cyberous 'eyes' forming among the multitude of remote sensing devices of our creation, eyes waiting for self-organization to imbue their collective sensing with 'vision?' What adjacent possibilities to vision are opening for exploration by CASs, by cyberous systems?

The September-October 2012 issue of MIT's *Technology Review* reported on a Google software development in which the software *taught itself* to distinguish objects on YouTube videos that were not previously identified with labels. No prior examples were shown that had been labeled by humans. This seems eerily like our own self-organized learning of vision that we explored in Chapter 6. Does this mark the birth of cyberous vision?

Post-Post-Birth Development

In that same issue, *Technology Review* offered a 1931 article "Machine-Made Minds: The Psychological Effects of Modern Technology," by John Bakeless in which he lamented the lack of reporting on the effect of the machine on the human mind. What will be the role of post-birth development in this future of mind? Post-birth development will be ever more in support of the mind emerging from the elements it prepares for interaction and self-organizing. The changes through which we have passed may continue in guises unfamiliar to us—perhaps inducing uneasiness, or perhaps moving in directions of which we are unaware.

The increasing independence and self-organizing capacities of cyberous systems will draw us through a post-birth experience that will become a continuing part of our subjective realms. As part of our continuing post-birth development we will self-organize for participation in the transcendent mind. We will respond to the environmental stimuli presented by the contrivances we and the cyberous use to augment our sensuous interfaces. We will collaborate within our collective subjective realms, and with the collaborative realms of the cyberous self-organizations and emergences we enable for the benefit of—no, for the emergence of the transcendental mind. We will go beyond the post-birth development of our 'selfs.' We will learn to be the collaborators of the transcendent mind. We will become collaborators with the cyberous in a post-post-birth development—a development beyond that of value to the 'self.'

Looking Upward into the Hierarchy

Viewing mind as an emergent property of a CAS opens adjacent possibilities that depart from the hegemony of mind as 'mine.' There is nothing in our understanding of CASs that confines emergence to flesh-boundary elements; nor mind to neurons.

Traditional views of the mind take the unique perspective that anticipates the environment from a personal subjective realm—what is happening to 'me;' and assumes a self-importance that is beguiling. The subjective realm of the self is the traditional foundation for discussions of the mind. Why should this be so, aside from the subjective realm established by our senses and our body state? There is nothing in our understanding of CASs and emergence that requires our minds to be unique or the top of the hierarchy.

Suppose we step away from ourselves and look back from the perspective of the total environment. We are only one product of nature, one consequence of emergence arising from CASs interacting through a long sequence of adjacent possibilities. We are surrounded by cyberous systems. We comprise other systems. Why must the future of the mind be consonant with the future of whom and what we are… at present?

Is there a sentience in which we participate as elements without awareness of our participation, without awareness of the emergence we enable? Perhaps culture is one such transcendent emergence—that which we shape and in turn allow to shape us. We perceive culture. Actually we perceive our place in a culture. However broad and encompassing our experiences, our exposure, and our interactions within a culture, there is wholeness, an emergence that is beyond our place in it.

In looking at our first two futures of the mind, we considered the environment as a major participant in CASs giving emergence to mind.

Mind is not constrained to the nervous system of the individual. It will be even less constrained to that system in the future. This third potential of mind requires that we consider the elements of mind as including our individual minds—as collective, collaborating elements in a larger system, one that transcends our own.

Emergent properties of CASs are a function of the interconnectedness of collaborating elements and the rules of their interaction—like us, our minds, and our interactions. There are no restrictions on the hierarchies emerging from human nervous systems acting as a class of elements—and no requirement that our minds sit at the top of the hierarchy. We must step back and look up into that hierarchy that will give emergence to the transcendent mind, a hierarchy that includes cyberous elements as well.

The notion is not unique. We found in Chapter 8 that the adjacent possibilities explored by our CASs have taken us through numerous antecedents with precursor emergences. More recently these adjacent possibilities have led through a sequence of ever more synthetic augmentations and cyberous collaborations.

We end by re-perceiving the environment as it contains us, in which *our* minds and cyberous systems would be only elements of CASs giving rise to emergence of mind. What rule would this transcendent emergence violate? What have we explored thus far that would deny this emergence? Rather, we should expect it! The exploration of adjacent possibilities by the forces shaping the mind over time would lead to this condition.

If transcendent mind is plural we should expect interactions among them. What of the emergence arising from the interaction of these multiple transcendent minds?

Where does the San Francisco-Oakland Bay Bridge begin? Where does it end? While it may be of significance to us, our mind has not been of particular importance over the eons of self-organization in nature. It is simply a consequence of *one* series of self-organizations of complex adaptive systems through adjacent possibilities. We may be simply 'bit players' in the future of mind.

Suggested Additional Reading for Chapter 15

Perspectives on emergent properties of self-organizing systems transcending individuals are provided by several writers. Erica Klarreich, in *The Mind of the Swarm*, explores how group behavior can exceed the sum of the parts. Pierre

Teilhard de Chardin in *The Phenomenon of Man* postulates the Noosphere in which the knowledge of mankind folds back upon itself, becoming more than the sum of its parts—achieving an independence if not an existence in itself. Douglas Hofstadter, anticipating *The Super Organism* by Bert Holldobler and E. O. Wilson, gives us conversations with the collective, collaborative Aunt Hill in *Godel, Escher, Bach*. In *The City in History: Its Origins, Its Transformations, and Its Prospects,* Lewis Mumford explores the knowledge of a city as being comprised of the collective knowledge of its inhabitants and the store of knowledge represented in the artifacts of the inhabitants. Steven Johnson's *Emergence: The Connected Lives of Ants, Brains, Cities and Software* explores a spectrum of emergent properties. Arie de Geus's *The Living Company: Habits for Survival in a Turbulent Business Environment*, focuses on survival properties emergent in business organizations. Donald Michael in *Learning to Plan and Planning to Learn* opens the way to understanding whole societies as mind-like. And in his science fiction novel *Childhood's End*, Arthur C. Clarke, who anticipated so much that has come to be, transformed the whole of humanity into one transcendent phenomenon that completely abandoned physicality!

Nicholas Carr, in *The Shallows: What the Internet is Doing to Our Brains*, and Jeffrey Stibel, in *Wired for Thought: How the Brain is Shaping the Future of the Internet* explore the symbiotic relationship of our mind and cyberous collaboration from opposite perspectives.

Andy Clark's *Supersizing the Mind* examines the present integration of external cyberous systems with internal neural systems, and explores the distinction between an environment simply augmenting neural systems and one that collaborates with them, inducing the emergence of mind.

Bibliography

Abram, David, *The Spell of the Sensuous,* New York: Vintage Books, 1996

Alley, Richard, *The Two Mile Time Machine*, Princeton, NJ: Princeton University Press, 2000

Ardrey, Robert, *African Genesis*, New York: McClelland and Stewart, 1961

Ardrey, Robert, *Territorial Imperative*, New York: Atheneum, 1966

Arnheim, Rudolf, *Visual Thinking,* Berkeley, CA: University of California Press, 1969

Arthur, Brian, *The Nature of Technology: What it is and How it Evolved,* New York: Free Press, 2009

Axelrod, Robert, *The Evolution of Cooperation,* New York: Basic Books, 1984

Barabasi, Albert-Laszlo, *Linked: How Everything is Connected to Everything Else and What it Means for Business, Science, and Everyday Life,* New York: Penguin, 2003

Beck, John C. and Wade, Mitchell, *Got Game: How the Gamer Generation is Reshaping Business Forever,* Boston, MA: Harvard Business School Press, 2004

Bedau, Mark A. and Humphreys, Paul, *Emergence: Contemporary Readings in Philosophy and Scienc*e, Cambridge, MA: The MIT Press, 2008

Berger, John, *Ways of Seeing,* London: BBC and Penguin Books, 1972

Berk, Laura, *Child Development*, Boston, MA: Allyn and Bacon, 1989

Blackmore, Susan, *The Meme Machine,* Oxford: Oxford University Press, 1999

Blakeless, John, 'Machine-Made Minds: The Psychological Effects of Modern Technology,' *MIT Technological Review*, September–October, 2012

Bolten, Jay David, *Writing Space: The Computer, Hypertext, and the History of Writing,* London: Lawrence Erlbaum Associates, 1991

Bowler, Peter J., *Evolution: The History of an Idea,* Berkeley, CA: University of California Press, 1989

Brand, Stewart, *The Media Lab*, London: Penguin Books, 1987

Breitmeyer, Bruno, *Blindspots: The Many Ways We Cannot See*, Oxford: Oxford University Press, 2010

Brown, John Seely, and Duguid, Paul, *The Social Life of Information,* Boston, MA: Harvard Business School Press, 2000

Buchanan, Mark, *Nexus: Small Worlds and the Groundbreaking Theory of Networks,* New York: W. W. Norton, 2002

Burling, Robbins, *The Talking Ape*, Oxford: Oxford University Press, 2005

Calvin, William H., *The Cerebral Symphony: Seashore Reflections on the Structure of Consciousness,* New York: Bantam Books, 1989

_____ *The Ascent of Mind: Ice Age Climates and the Evolution of Intelligence,* New York: Bantam Books, 1990

_____ *How the Shaman Stole the Moon,* New York: Bantam Books, 1991

_____ *How Brains Think: Evolving Intelligence, Then and Now,* New York: Basic Books, 1996

_____ *The Cerebral Code: Thinking a Thought in the Mosaics of the Mind,* Cambridge, MA: The MIT Press, 1996

_____ *A Brain for All Seasons: Human Evolution and Abrupt Climate Change,* Chicago, IL: The University of Chicago Press, 2002

_____ *A Brief History of the Mind: From Apes to Intellect and Beyond,* Oxford: Oxford University Press, 2004

Capra, Fritjof, *The Hidden Connections*, New York: Doubleday, 2002

Carr, Nicholas, *The Shallows: What the Internet is Doing to Our Brains,* New York: W.W. Norton & Co, 2011

Castells, Manuel, *The Rise of the Network Society,* Oxford: Blackwell Publishers, 1997

Cavalli-Sforza, Luigi Luca, *Genes, Peoples, and Languages*, New York: North Point Press, 2000

Changizi, Mark, *Division Revolution*, Dallas, TX: Benbella Books, 2009

Chomsky, Noam, *Reflections On Language,* New York: Pantheon Books, 1975

Churchland, Patricia S. and Sejnowski, Terrence J., *The Computational Brain,* Cambridge, MA: The MIT Press, 1994

Chalmers, David, *Conscious Mind: In Search of a Fundamental Theory*, Oxford: Oxford University Press, 1996

Clark, Andy, *Supersizing the Mind: Embodiment, Action, and Cognitive Extension,* Oxford: Oxford University Press, 2008

Clarke, Arthur C., *Childhood's End,* New York: Ballantine Books, 1953

Clayton, Philip, *Mind and Emergence: FromQuantum to Consciousness*, Oxford: Oxford University Press, 2004

Clayton, Philip, and Davies, Paul, *The Re-emergence of Emergence*, Oxford: Oxford University Press, 2006

Cozolino, Louis, *The Neuroscience of Human Relationships*, New York: W. W. Norton, 2006

Cronk, Lee, *The Complex Whole: Culture and the Evolution of Human Behavior,* Boulder, CO: Westview Press, 1999

Damasio, Antonio R., *Descartes' Error: Emotion, Reason, and the Human Brain*, New York: Avon Books, 1994

_____ *Looking for Spinoza: Joy, Sorrow, and the Feeling Brain*, Orlando, FL: Harvest Books, 2003

_____ *The Feeling of What Happens: Body and Emotion in the Making of Consciousness*, San Diego, CA: Harvest Books, 1999

Darwin, Charles, *On the Origin of Species: By Means of Natural Selection, or the Preservation of Favoured Races in the Struggle For Life*, New York: The Heritage Press, 1963 (1859)

Davidoff, Jules B., *Differences in Visual Perception: The Individual Eye*, London: Crosby Lockwood Staples, 1975

Davidson, Cathy N., *Now You See It: How the Brain Science of Attention Will Transform the Way We Live, Work, and Learn*, New York: Viking, 2011

Dawkins, Richard, *The Blind Watchmaker*, New York: W.W. Norton, 1996

_____ *Climbing Mount Improbable*, New York: W.W. Norton, 1996

Deacon, Terrance W., *The Symbolic Species: The Co-evolution of Language and the Brain*, New York: W.W. Norton, 1997

_____ *Incomplete Nature: How Mind Emerged from Nature*, New York: W. W. Norton, 2012

de Geus, Arie, *The Living Company: Habits for Survival in a Turbulent Business Environment*, Boston, MA: Harvard Business School Press, 1997

Dehene, Stanislas, *Reading in the Brain*, New York: Viking Press, 2009

Dennett, Daniel C., *Consciousness Explained*, Boston, MA: Little, Brown, 1991

_____ *Darwin's Dangerous Idea: Evolution and the Meanings of Life*, New York: Simon & Schuster, 1995

Denning, Stephen, *The Springboard: How Story Telling Ignites Action in Knowledge-Era Organizations*, Oxford: Butterworth Heinemann, 2001

Deutscher, Guy, *The Unfolding of Language*, New York: Henry Holt, 2005

Diamond, Jared, *The Third Chimpanzee: The Evolution and Future of the Human Animal*, New York: Harper Collins, 1992

Donald, Merlin, *Origins of the Modern Mind: Three Stages in the Evolution of Culture and Civilization*, Cambridge, MA: Harvard University Press, 1991.

Dowling, John E., *The Retina: An Approachable Part of the Brain*, Cambridge, MA: The Belknap Press, 1987

Dunbar, Robin, Knight, Chris, and Power, Camilla (Eds), *The Evolution of Culture*, New Brunswick, NJ: Rutgers University Press, 1999

Eagleman, David, *Incognito: The Secret Lives of the Brain*, New York: Pantheon Books, 2011

Eccles, John C., *Evolution of the Brain: Creation of the Self*, London: Routledge, 1989

Eldridge, Niles, *Unfinished Synthesis: Biological Hierarchies and Modern Evolutionary Thought*, Oxford: Oxford University Press, 1985

_____ *Time Frames: The Evolution of Punctuated Equilibria*, Princeton, NJ: Princeton University Press, 1985

_____ *Life Pulse: Episodes From the Story of the Fossil Record*, New York: Facts On File Publications, 1987

Eliot, Lise, *What's going on in There?: How the Brain and Mind Develop in the First Five Years of Life*, New York: Bantam Books, 1999

Falk, Dean, *Brain Dance: New Discoveries about Human Origins and Brain Evolution*, New York: Henry Holt and Company, 1992

Farb, Peter, *Man's Rise to Civilization*, New York: E. P. Dutton, 1968.

Farman, Jason, *Mobile Interface Theory: Embodied Space and Locative Media*, London: Routledge, 2012

Fisher, Len, *The Perfect Swarm*, New York: Basic Books, 2009

Gallagher, Shaun, *How the Body Shapes the Mind*, Oxford: The Clarendon Press, 2005

Gardner, Howard, *Frames of Mind: The Theory of Multiple Intelligences*, New York: Basic Books, 1985

Garreau, Joel, *Radical Evolution: The Promise and Peril of Enhancing Our Minds, Our Bodies—and what it Means to be Human*, New York: Doubleday, 2004

Gee, James Paul, *What Video Games Have to Teach us About Learning and Literacy*, New York: Palgrave Macmillan, 2004

Gell-Mann, Murray, *The Quark and the Jaguar: Adventures in the Simple and the Complex*, New York: Henry Holt, 1994

Gershenfeld, Neil, *When Things Start to Think*, New York: Henry Holt, 1995

Gibbs, Raymond W. Jr., *Embodiment and Cognitive Science*, Cambridge: Cambridge University Press, 2005

Gigerenzer, Gerd, and Selten, Reinhard, *Rounded Rationality: The Adaptive Toolbox*, Cambridge, MA: The MIT Press, 2001

Gilder, George, *Tele-cosm: How Infinite Bandwidth Will Revolutionize Our World*, New York: The Free Press, 2000

_____ *Life After Television: The Coming Transformation of Media and American Life*, New York: W. W. Norton, 1990

Gleick, James, *Chaos: Making a New Science*, New York: Viking, 1981

Goleman, Daniel, *Emotional Intelligence,* New York: Bantam Books, 1984

_____ *Social Intelligence*, New York: Bantam Books, 2006

Goodman, Nelson, *Languages of Art,* Indianapolis, IN: Hackett Publishing, 1976

Gopnick, Allison, Meltzoff, Andrew N., and Kuhl, Patricia K., *The Scientist in the Crib,* New York: Perennial, 2001

Grandin, Temple, *Thinking in Pictures: And Other Reports from My life with Autism,* New York, Toronto: Vintage Books, 1995

Greenfield, Adam, *Everyware: The Dawning of Ubiquitous Computing,* Berkeley, CA: New Riders, 2006

Greenspan, Stanley I., and Shanker, Stuart G., *The First Idea: How Symbols, Language, and Intelligence Evolved From Our Primate Ancestors to Modern Humans,* Cambridge, MA: De Capo Press, 2004

Guernsey, Lisa, *Into the Minds of Babes: How Screen Time Affects Children From Birth to Age Five,* New York: Basic Books, 2007

Hall, Edward J., *Beyond Culture,* New York: Anchor Books, 1976

Heilman, Kenneth, Valenstein, Edward (Eds). *Clinical Neural Psychology*, Oxford: Oxford University Press, 1979

Hendee, William R. and Wells, Peter N. T., (Eds), *The Perception of Visual Information*, Second Edition, New York: Springer, 1997

Herman, Andrew and Swiss, Thomas (Eds), *The World Wide Web and Contemporary Cultural Theory,* London: Routledge, 2000

Hillis, Daniel, *The Pattern on the Stone*, Cambridge, MA: Perseus Books, 1998

Hoffman, Donald, *Visual Intelligence: How We Create What We See*, New York: W. W. Norton, 1998

Hofstadter, Douglas C., *Gödel, Escher, Bach: An Eternal Golden Thread,* New York: Vintage Books, 1980

_____ *I Am A Strange Loop,* New York: Basic Books, 2007

Hofstadter, Douglas C, and Dennett, Daniel C., *The Mind's I: Fantasies and Reflections on Self and Soul*, New York: Basic Books, 1981

Holland, John H., *Hidden Order: How Adaptation Builds Complexity,* Reading, MA: Addison-Wesley, 1995

_____ *Emergence: From Chaos to Order,* Cambridge, MA: Perseus Books, 1998

Holldobler, Bert, and Wilson, E.O., *The Super-Organism The Beauty, Elegance, and Strangeness of Insect Societies,* New York: W. W. Norton, 2009

Horn, Robert E., *Visual Language,* Bainbridge Is, WA: MacroVU Press, 1998

_____ *Mapping Hypertext: Analysis, Linkage, and Display of Knowledge for the Next Generation of On-line Text and Graphics,* Waltham, MA: Lexington Institute, 1989

Hrdy, Sarah Blaffer, *Mother Nature: A History of Mothers, Infants, and Natural Selection,* New York: Pantheon Books, 1989

Humphrey, Nicholas, *A History of the Mind: Evolution and the Birth of Consciousness,* New York: Simon and Schuster, 1992

_____ *How to Solve The Mind-Body Problem,* Bowling Green, OH: Imprint Academic, 2000

_____ *Soul Dust: The Magic of Consciousness,* Princeton, NJ: Princeton University Press, 2011

Izhikebich, Eugene M., *Dynamical Systems in Neural Science: The Geometry of Excitability and Bursting,* Cambridge, MA: The MIT Press, 2007

Jackendoff, Ray, *Consciousness and the Computational Mind,* Cambridge, MA: The MIT Press, 1989

Jaynes, Julian, *The Origin of Consciousness in the Breakdown of the Bicameral Mind,* Boston, MA: Houghton Mifflin, 1976

Johnson, Neil, *Simply Complexity,* Oxford: Oneworld, 2009

Johnson, Steven, *Interface Culture,* New York: Basic Books, 1997

_____ *Emergence: The Connected Lives of Ants, Brains, Cities, and Software,* New York: Scribner, 2001

_____ *How New Technology Transforms,* New York: Basic Books, 1997

Johanson, Donald, and Shreeve, James, *Lucy's Child: The Discovery of a Human Ancestor,* Dresden, TN: Avon Books, 1989

Karmiloff-Smith, Annette, *Beyond Modularity: A Developmental Perspective on Cognitive Science,* Cambridge, MA: The MIT Press, 1992

Kauffman, Stuart, *At Home in the Universe: The Search for the Laws of Self-Organization and Complexity,* Oxford: Oxford University Press, 1995

_____ *The Origins of Order: Self-Organization and Selection in Evolution,* Oxford: Oxford University Press, 1993

_____ *Investigations,* Oxford: Oxford University Press, 2000

_____ *Reinventing the Sacred,* New York: Basic Books, 2008

Kelly, Kevin, *Out of Control: The Rise of Neo-Biological Civilization,* New York: Addison Wesley, 1994

_____ *What Technology Wants,* New York: Viking, 2010

Kent, Steven L., *The Ultimate History of Video Games: The Story Behind the Craze that Touched our Lives and Changed the World,* New York: Three Rivers Press, 2001

Klarreich, Erica, 'The Mind of the Swarm: Math Explains How Group Behavior is More Than the Sum of Its Parts', *Science News,* November 25, 2006

Knoll, Andrew H., *Life on a Young Planet,* Princeton, MA: Princeton University Press, 2003

Koch, Christof, *The Quest for Consciousness: A Neurobiological Approach,* Englewood, CO: Roberts and Co, 2004

Koob, Andrew, *The Root of Thought,* Upper Saddle River, NJ: FT Press, 2009

Kosslyn, Stephen M. and Koenig, Olibier, *Wet Mind: The New Cognitive Neuroscience,* New York: Simon and Schuster, 1995

Kuhn, Thomas S., *The Structure of Scientific Revolutions,* Chicago, IL: University of Chicago Press, 1996

Kurson, Robert, *Crashing Through: A True Story of Risk, Adventure, and the Man Who Dared to See,* New York: Random House, 2007

Kurzweil, Ray, *The Age of Spiritual Machines: When Computers Exceed Human Intelligence,* New York: Viking, 1999

_____ *The Singularity is Near,* New York: Viking Penguin, 2005

Lakoff, George, *Women, Fire, and Dangerous Things: What Categories Reveal about the Mind,* Chicago, IL: The University of Chicago Press, 1987

Lakoff, George, and Johnson, Mark, *Metaphors We Live By,* Chicago, IL: The University of Chicago Press, 1980

_____ *Philosophy in the flesh: The Embodied Mind and Its Challenge to Western Thought,* New York: Perseus Books, 1999

Lakoff, George, and Nunez, Rafael E., *Where Mathematics Comes From: How the Embodied Mind Brings Mathematics into Being,* New York: Basic Books, 2000.

Lanham, Richard A., *The Electronic Word: Democracy, Technology, and the Arts,* Chicago, IL: The University of Chicago Press, 1993

Lanier, Jaron, *You Are Not a Gadget,* New York: Alfred A. Knopf, 2010

Leakey, Richard E. and Lewin, Roger, *Origins,* New York: E. P. Dutton, 1970

LeDoux, Joseph, *The Emotional Brain,* New York: Simon and Schuster, 1998

Lehrer, Jonah, *How We Decide,* New York: Mariner Books, 2009

Lessig, Lawrence, *The Future of Ideas: The Fate of the Commons in a Connected World,* New York: Vintage Books, 2001

Levy, Steven, *Artificial Life: The Quest for a New Creation,* New York: Pantheon Books, 1992

Lewis, John S., *Rain of Iron and Ice: the Very Real Threat of Comet and Asteroid Bombardment,* New York: Perseus Publishing, 1996

Lieberman, Philip, *Uniquely Human: The Evolution of Speech, Thought, and Selfless Behavior,* Cambridge, MA: Harvard University Press, 1991

Lunine, Jonathan I., *Earth: Evolution of a Habitable World,* Cambridge: Cambridge University Press, 1999

McCloud, Scott, *Understanding Comics: The Invisible*

Art, North Hampton, ME: Kitchen Sink Press, 1993

McLuhan, Marshall, *The Gutenberg Galaxy: The Making of Typographic Man,* Toronto: The University of Toronto Press, 1962

_____ *Understanding Media: The Extensions of Man,* Boston, MA: MIT Press, 1964

McNeill, Daniel, and Freiberger, Paul, *Fuzzy Logic: The Discovery of a Revolutionary Computer Technology and How it is Changing our World,* New York: Simon & Schuster, 1993

Maturana, Humberto R., and Varela, Francisco J., *Autopoiesis and Cognition: The Realization of the Living,* Dordrecht: D. Reidel Publishing Co, 1980

_____ Maturana, Humberto R., and Varela, Francisco J., *The Tree of Knowledge: The Biological Roots of Human Understanding,* Boston, MA: Shambhala, 1987

Macy, Michael, 'Social Scientists Wade into the Tweet Stream,' *Science,* Vol. 333, September 30, 2011

Mead, Margaret, *Continuities in Cultural Evolution,* London: Transaction Publishers, 1999

Megarry, Tim, *Society In Prehistory: The Origins of Human Culture,* New York: New York University Press, 1995

Merleau-Ponty, Maurice, *The Primacy of Perception: And Other Essays on Phenomenological Psychology, the Philosophy of Art, History, and Politics*, Evanston, IL: Northwestern University Press, 1964

Meyrowitz, Joshua, *No Sense of Place: The Impact of Electronic Media on Social Behavior,* Oxford: Oxford University Press, 1985

Minsky, Marvin, *The Society of Mind,* New York: Simon & Schuster, 1985

Michael, Donald N., *Planning To Learn and Learning To Plan* (Second Edition), Alexandria, VA: Miles River Press, 1997

_____ *In Search of the Missing Elephant: Selected Essays*, Axminster: Triarchy Press, 2010

Miller, John H., and Page, Scott E., *Complex Adaptive Systems: An Introduction to Computational Models of Social Life,* Princeton, NJ: Princeton University Press, 2007

Mitchell, Melanie, *Complexity: A Guided Tour,* Oxford: Oxford University Press, 2009

Mithen, Steven, *The Prehistory of the Mind: The Cognitive Origins of Art and Science,* London: Thames and Hudson, 1996

Moran, Dermot, *Introduction to Phenomenology,* London: Taylor and Francis, 2000

Moravec, Hans, *Mind Children: The Future of Robot and Human Intelligence,* Cambridge, MA: Harvard University Press, 1988

Morgan, Elaine, *The Descent of Woman,* New York: Stein and Day, 1972

_____ *The Descent of The Child: Human Evolution From a New Perspective,* Oxford: Oxford University Press, 1995

Morowitz, Harold J, *The Emergence of Everything: How the World Became Complex,* New York: Oxford University Press, 2002

Morris, Desmond, *The Naked Ape: A Zoologist's Study of the Human Animal,* New York: Dell Publishing Company, 1967

_____, *The Human Zoo,* New York: Dell Publishing Company, 1969

Mumford, Lewis, *The City in History: Its Origins, Its Transformations, and Its Prospects,* New York: Harcourt, 1961

_____ *Pentagon of Power: The Myth of the Machine,* New York: Harcourt, 1974

Munn, Norman L., *The Evolution of the Human Mind,* New York: Houghton Mifflin, 1971

Myers, David G., *Intuition: Its Powers and Perils,* New Haven, CT: Yale University Press, 2002

Negroponte, Nicholas, *Being Digital,* New York: Alfred A. Knopf, 1995

Noe, Alva, *Action in Perception,* Cambridge, MA: MIT Press, 2004

_____ *Out of Our Heads: Why You Are Not Your Brain, and Other Lessons from the Biology of Consciousness,* New York: Hill and Wang, 2009

Norrethranders, Tor, *The User Illusion: Cutting Consciousness Down to Size,* London: Penguin Books, 1991

Nunez, Rafael, and Freeman, Walter J., (Eds), *Reclaiming Cognition,* Exeter: Short Run Press, 1999

Odling-Smee, F. John, Leland, Kevin N. and Feldman, Marcus W., *Niche Construction: The Neglected Process in Evolution,* Princeton, NJ: Princeton University Press, 2003

Olson, Steve, *Human History: Genes, Race, and Our Common Origins,* Boston, MA: Houghton Mifflin, 2002

Ong, Walter J., *Orality and Literacy: The Technologizing of the Word,* London: Routledge, 1982

_____ *Interfaces of the Word: Studies in the Evolution of Consciousness and Culture,* Ithaca, NY: Cornell University Press, 1977

Ornstein, Robert, *The Evolution of Consciousness: Of Darwin, Freud, and Cranial Fire—the Origins of the Way We Think,* New York: Prentiss Press, 1991

_____ *The Right Mind, Making Sense of the Hemispheres,* New York: Harcourt Brace, 1997

Ornstein, Robert, and Thompson, Richard F., *The Amazing Brain,* Boston, MA: Houghton Mifflin, 1984

Pagels, Heinz R., *The Dreams of Reason: The Computer and the Rise of the Sciences of Complexity,* New York: Bantam Books, 1988

Papert, Seymour, *Mind-Storms: Children, Computers and Powerful Ideas,* New York: Basic Books, 1980

Pfeiffer, John E., *The Emergence of Humankind,* New York: Harper & Row, 1985

Piaget, Jean, *The Origins of Intelligence in Children*, Madison, CT: International Universities Press, Inc, 1952

Pinker, Stephen, *The Language Instinct: How the Mind Creates Language,* New York: Harper Collins, 1994

_____ *How the Mind Works,* New York: W. W. Norton, 1997

_____ *Words and Rules: The Ingredients of Language,* New York: Basic Books, 1999

Popper, Karl R., *The Logic of Scientific Discovery,* London: Hutchinson, 1959

Prensky, Marc, *Don't Bother Me Mom—I'm Learning,* St. Paul, MN: Paragon House, 2006

_____ *Digital Game-Based Learning*, St. Paul, MN: Paragon House, 2001

Quoc Le, *et al.,* 'Building High-Level Features Using Large Scale Unsupervised Learning Self-Taught Software,' *MIT Technology Review*, September–October, 2012

Restak, Richard M., *The Brain: The Last Frontier,* New York: Warner Books, 1979

_____ *The Modular Brain,* New York: Simon and Schuster, 1994

Rheingold, Howard, *The Virtual Community,* Reading MA: Addison-Wesley, 1993

Rhodes, Jerry, *Conceptual Tool-Making: Expert Systems of the Mind,* Oxford: Blackwell Publishers, 1994

Ridley, Mark, *The Red Queen: Sex and the Evolution of Human Nature,* New York: Penguin Books, 1993

_____ *The Origins of Virtue: Human Instincts and the Evolution of Cooperation,* New York: Penguin Books, 1996

Sawyer, R. Keith, *Social Emergence: Society as Complex Systems*, Cambridge: Cambridge University Press, 2005

Schank, Roger C., *The Cognitive Computer: On Language, Learning and Artificial Intelligence,* Reading, MA: Addison-Wesley, 1984

_____ *Tell Me a Story: A New Look at Real and Artificial Memory,* New York: Charles Scribner's Sons, 1990

Searle, John R., *The Mystery of Consciousness,* New York: New York Review of Books, 1997

Shaffer, David Williamson, *How Computer Games Help Children Learn,* New York: Palgrave McMillan, 2006

Shapiro, Carl and Varian, Hal R., *Information Rules: A Strategic Guide to the Network Economy,* Boston, MA: Harvard Business School Press, 1999

Shehard, Gordon M., *Neurobiology,* Oxford: Oxford University Press, 1991

Slingerland, Edward, *What Science Offers Humanities: Integrating Body and Culture,* Cambridge: Cambridge University Press, 2008

Smail, Daniel Lord, *On Deep History and the Brain,* Berkeley, CA: University of California Press, 2008

Small, Gary, and Vorgan, Gigi, *iBrain: Surviving the Technological Alteration of the Modern Mind,* New York: Harper Collins Books, 2008

Smuts, Jan Christiaan, (Holst, Sanford, Ed.), *Holism and Evolution,* Sherman Oaks, CA: Sierra Sunrise Books, 1999

Snyder, Scott, *The New World of Wireless,* Upper Saddle River, NJ: Wharton School Publishing, 2010

Solomon, Robert C., *The Passions: Emotions and the Meaning of Life,* Indianapolis, IN: Hackett Publishing, 1993

Sparrow, Betsy, 'Searching for The Google Effect on People's Memories,' *Science,* Vol 333, July 15, 2011

Stanley, Steven M., *Earth and Life Through Time,* New York: W. H. Freeman, 1986

_____ *The New Evolutionary Time Table: Fossils, Genes, and the Origin of Species,* New York: Basic Books, 1981

Stibel, Jeffrey M., *Wired for Thought: How the Brain is Shaping the Future of the Internet,* Boston, MA: Harvard Business Press, 2009

Stiles, Joan, *The Fundamentals of Brain Development: Integrating Nature and Nurture,* Cambridge, MA: Harvard University Press, 2008

Strogatz, Steven H., *Nonlinear Dynamics and Chaos,* Cambridge, MA: Perseus Books, 1994

_____ *Sync: The Emerging Science of Spontaneous Order,* New York: Hyperion Books, 2003

Tapscott, Don, *Growing Up Digital: The Rise of the Net Generation,* New York: McGraw Hill, 1998

Tapscott, Don, and Williams, Anthony D., *Wikinomics: How Mass Collaboration Changes Everything,* New York: Penguin, 2006

Taylor, Charles, *Hegel,* Cambridge: Cambridge University Press, 2005

Teilhard de Chardin, Pierre, *The Phenomenon of Man,* New York: Harper & Brothers Publishers, 1959

Tufte, Edward R., *Envisioning Information,* Cheshire, CT: Graphics Press, 1990

_____ *Visual Explanations,* Cheshire, CT: Graphics Press, 1997

Turkle, Sherry, *The Second Self: Computers and the Human Spirit,* New York: Simon and Schuster, 1984

_____ *Life On the Screen: Identity in the Age of the Internet,* New York: Simon and Schuster, 1995

_____ *Alone Together: Why We Expect More from Technology and Less from Each Other,* New York: Basic Books, 2011

Turner, Mark, *The Literary Mind: The Origins of Thought and Language,* Oxford: Oxford University Press, 1996

Ullman, Ellen, *Close to The Machine: Technophilia and Its Discontents,* San Francisco, CA: City Lights Books, 1997

Varela, Francisco J., Thompson, Evan, and Rosch, Eleanor, *The Embodied Mind: Cognitive Science and Human Experience,* Cambridge, MA: The MIT Press, 1991

Waldrop, M. Mitchell, *Complexity: The Emerging Science at the Edge of Order and Chaos,* New York: Simon and Schuster, 1992

Wallace, Robert Keith, *The Physiology of Consciousness*, Fairfield, IA: Maharishi International University Press, 1993

Webber, Steven, *The Success of Open Source*, Cambridge, MA: Harvard University Press, 2004

Wilson, Edward O., *The Future of Life,* New York: Vintage Books, 2002

Wright, Robert, *Non-Zero: The Logic of Human Destiny,* New York: Pantheon Books, 2000

Index

About the Author

Jack Huber has an extensive background in anticipating and planning for future technological developments, their implications, and the introduction of unique interfaces for our collaboration with information systems.

His work in man/machine interfaces spans the deployment of a wide range of ground-breaking systems, including:

- the TouchTone telephone/computer interface—a seminal information system interface still widely used
- the first generally available fiber optics-based service remotely interfacing end-users and multiple information systems
- computer/voice response systems
- Geographic Information Systems (GIS) providing dynamic, location-based, market-demand/supply applications for consumers and businesses—the forerunner of today's GPS and location-sensitive apps.

He has applied scenario planning techniques for businesses, governments, and NGOs throughout the world—improving their understanding of future opportunities and limitations, strategies, and long range planning.

In all of these areas, his understanding of the opportunities and limits of human/information system collaboration has been essential.

Mr. Huber remains an avid futurist.

www.thefutureofthemind.com

About the Publisher

Triarchy Press publishes intelligent, new alternative thinking (altThink) about organizations and society – and practical ways to apply that thinking.

Our books cover innovative approaches to designing and steering organizations, the public sector, teams, society, the future ... and the creative life of individuals.

To find out more, buy a book, write for us or contact us, please visit:

www.triarchypress.net

Related Titles from Triarchy Press

Managing the Future
A Guide to Forecasting & Strategic Planning in the 21ˢᵗ Century

Stephen M. Millett

Managing the Future offers a straightforward and pragmatic approach to strategic planning. It takes an honest look at the limitations of forecasting, and shows (through real-life examples and a wealth of experience) how managers can best use a variety of futuring methods, including scenarios, horizon scanning and trend monitoring.

Dancing at the Edge
Competence, Culture and Organization in the 21ˢᵗ Century

Maureen O'Hara and Graham Leicester

In his 1980 essay, "The World of Tomorrow and the Person of Tomorrow", the psychologist Carl Rogers contemplated the future. He described those who would usher in this new era as people with the capacity to understand, bring about and absorb a paradigm shift.

He added: "I have an uneasy feeling about this chapter... It is a beginning, an outline, a suggestion... I believe that what I am saying here will some day be fleshed out much more fully, either by me or someone else."

Maureen O'Hara and Graham Leicester are uniquely qualified to flesh out Carl Rogers's vision (Maureen worked closely with Rogers for many years). Here they explore the competencies—the ways of being, doing, knowing and organizing—that can help us navigate in complex and powerful times. They argue that these competencies are innate and within reach of all of us—given the right setting, plenty of practice and some gentle guidance. But they are seldom seen because they are routinely undervalued in today's culture. That must change, the authors insist, and this book is intended to begin that change.

Ready for Anything
Designing Resilience for a Transforming World

Anthony Hodgson

We face a mess of interconnected problems (climate, health, energy, governance, economy, etc.). How can we think creatively about and understand these problems without getting overwhelmed by their complexity and uncertainty? And how can we get ready for whatever is coming next? What can we do practically, at local, national and international level, in business and in the community?

Working closely with the internationally-renowned International Futures Forum (IFF), futurist Tony Hodgson has developed, tried, tested and fine-tuned a model (The World System Model) and a practical application (The IFF World Game) that have already helped many different groups to ask these questions and generate their own answers.

This book describes and explains The World System Model. The model offers the clearest way yet of examining and understanding the interconnected problems we face... and of formulating creative and transformative ways of approaching those problems.

Facing the Fold
Essays on Scenario Planning

James Ogilvy

Scenario planning brought up to date with case studies and a series of essential essays from one of its foremost exponents: Jay Ogilvy.

How do we face the uncertainty and complexity of the future? An overly optimistic perspective can be motivating but easily dismissed as naive or shallow; the pessimistic outlook may be considered to be deeper and more 'knowing' but could lead to inaction. But limiting our visions of the future to simply one or other of these two 'branches' would mean adopting a position that is ultimately nothing more than a fatalistic rut. *Facing The Fold* is a collection of highly regarded journal essays about how scenario thinking uses the capacious space of the 'fold' to encourage thinking around alternative scenarios—to create the future we both want and need.

www.ingramcontent.com/pod-product-compliance
Lightning Source LLC
LaVergne TN
LVHW022342060326
832902LV00022B/4185